C000157987

More About Acting

BY THE SAME AUTHOR

About Acting
First Houses

More About Acting ~

~ PETER BARKWORTH

Secker & Warburg
London

First published in England 1984 by
Martin Secker & Warburg Limited
54 Poland Street, London W1V 3DF

Copyright © Peter Barkworth 1984

British Library Cataloguing in Publication Data

Barkworth, Peter
  More about acting.
  1. Acting
  I. Title
  792'.028   PN2065

ISBN 0–436–03293–7
ISBN 0–436–03294–5 (pbk.)

Quotations are printed by kind permission of the following:
Ian Watson, *Conversations with Ayckbourn*: Macdonald &
Company Ltd; John Keay, *Eccentric Travellers*: John Murray Ltd
and BBC Publications; Brendan Behan, *The Hostage*: Methuen,
London; Christopher Fry, *Venus Observed* (1950), Oxford
University Press. The extract from *The Apple Cart* is reprinted
by permission of the Society of Authors on behalf of the
Bernard Shaw Estate.

Typeset by Deltatype, Ellesmere Port
Printed and bound in Great Britain by
Richard Clay (The Chaucer Press) Limited
Bungay, Suffolk

To
Judi Dench
Alec McCowen
Edward Petherbridge
Anna Massey
Wyn Jones
Alison Steadman
Patience Collier
Roger Rees
Prunella Scales
Peter Plouviez

This book is enlarged, in scope as well as in size, on account of their contributions to it. I wouldn't have done without them for anything. I am grateful for their opinions, and for the tales of their experiences which, in many instances, have been so very different from my own.

Contents

How Do I Work On A Part?   **170**

**This Is What Happens When You Go
Filming**   **176**

Odds And Ends   **190**

Maxims   **203**

Index   **205**

Out Of Work ~

I had arrived at the last room of the *Picasso's Picassos* exhibition at the Hayward Gallery. No one else was there except an attendant who was sitting in a far corner, reading a book. My shoes squeaked on the tiled floor as I wandered round the pictures and sculptures, trying to concentrate. It was a brighter room than the others, with skylights and a view over the river. But I'd had enough and wanted to go. The idea of walking briskly across Waterloo Bridge in the hazy winter sunshine and having lunch somewhere in Covent Garden seemed infinitely preferable to staying there any longer.

The attendant turned a page and looked up. Some more people came into the room. Right, I'm off, I thought. But the attendant was standing now with a vague look of recognition on his face. I don't know him, do I? I wondered. He made straight for me, right across the room. Damn, I thought. I really did want to go.

"Hello," he said, hushed, not wanting to distract the new arrivals.

"Hello," I said, equally hushed but more impatiently than I had intended.

"Don't you remember me?"

"Erm . . ."

"We met in that pub opposite the Cambridge Theatre during the interval of *One Mo' Time*. I was with Marianne Bates."

"Oh, of course," I said, only barely remembering.

1

Marianne was a mutual friend and had done most of the talking. "What are you doing here?"

"Well," he said slowly, "trying to make ends meet, actually."

Oh that's right, he's an actor. I remembered he'd said so. He was about twenty-five, I guessed, and was tall and had straight fair hair.

"Is work bad at the moment?" I asked.

"Terrible," he said, and smiled, and looked around.

"When did you last have a job?"

"Well . . . I did a couple of plays at Northampton about six months ago."

God, what a profession, I thought. "A long time," I said.

"Yes," he said. "Feels endless. It's just getting started again . . ."

"In London, you mean?"

"Yes. Well anywhere really . . ."

"Yes."

". . . because I think I'm all right: I mean I got good notices and people said nice things." He looked quite bewildered for a moment. "Never mind," he said, "I've got an interview for a beer commercial the day after tomorrow, so that's something. But I don't suppose I'll get it: there are always hordes of people there. And I'm up for a small part in *Juliet Bravo* in about three weeks. My agent says it sounds an ideal part for me, so I'm afraid I'm pinning a lot of hopes on it. Mustn't, though."

"You can't help it, though, can you?" I said. "Would it be your first telly?"

"First for the BBC. I had a tiny part for Granada about two years ago."

"I hope you get it."

"Thank you," he said. And then: "I must tell you. I meant to tell you the other evening but I was too shy. I've read *About Acting*. A friend of mine lent me his copy. It's very good."

"Thank you," I said.

"The only thing is . . . I don't know if I should say this . . ."

"What?"

"He said, this friend of mine, that your book was all very well if you've got work, but it doesn't tell you anything about how to get it, does it?"

"No," I conceded, "he's right, it doesn't. It wasn't meant to. It was just meant to be about what it says it's about. And I'm not sure if you can tell people about how to get jobs. There's no golden formula."

"I know," he said. "But although being out of work has nothing to do with acting, it has a great deal to do with the average actor's life. Don't you think?"

"Yes," I said. "Yes, it has. Unfortunately."

"Anyway, that's what my friend said."

"Yes," I said. "Thank you. And good luck with the interviews."

"Fingers crossed," he said, and went back to his corner.

And I walked back over Waterloo Bridge more slowly than I had thought I would.

*

Several months after that I went to Equity's offices in Harley Street to ask Peter Plouviez, the General Secretary, for a few facts and figures.

"Well," he said, picking up a lightweight office chair and bringing it round his desk so that we could talk more easily above the clatter of his assistant's typewriter, "let's get the numbers in perspective first. There are about 30,000 members of Equity. But of these 6,000 are Variety performers and over 4,000 of the rest are not actors: they are stage managers, opera singers, ballet dancers, television presenters, broadcasters, directors, designers, extras and so on."

"So there are fewer than 20,000 actors on your books?"

"Yes."

"And on any given day about how many of those actors would you say are not working?"

"Between sixty and seventy per cent. But figures for this can be misleading on account of the sporadic nature of an actor's work. For example, someone may be working for a film on a daily rate. The fact that he is used, say, on only one day in a

3

week, and in some weeks not at all, hardly puts him in the same category as someone who is completely out of work. The same applies to people who do commercials, or commentaries or broadcasts."

"But unemployment is still a major problem? There are still too many actors chasing too few jobs?"

"Oh yes. Yes," he said, "it's an ever-present problem. So we have to try and keep the numbers down to a reasonable level. That's why we introduced the Control of Entry scheme. It seemed the fairest way. We have to protect, as far as we can, the job prospects of our existing members. I think it's worked out quite well, really. It isn't that we prevent talented young people from joining the Union: we've just made it that little bit harder."

"You mean by restricting the allocation of Equity cards and by imposing the forty weeks of provisional membership to start with?"

"Yes."

"There are some absurd anomalies in all this, though, aren't there?" I said. "A new member has to have forty weeks of employment under his belt before he is allowed to have a part in the West End or on a Number One tour, but can appear in a leading role on television straight away."

"Yes. It's silly. Silly. It's the result of different negotiations with different bodies at different times. We have to get what we can when we can. There's a long way to go . . ." He relit his pipe and asked if I would like a cup of trade union coffee.

"Thank you," I said. It was a hot day and I'd taken off my jacket and loosened my tie. He was wearing a dark pinstripe suit and kept his jacket on.

"Let's have two coffees, Anita, please," he said, and got up and looked out of the window at the view of all the other windows, walls and chimneys which he knew so well. "We can just see the top of the Langham," he said, pointing it out to me. It was quiet now in the merciful lull from the incessant typing. "When I came here over a hundred years ago there were only 8,000 members. But it wasn't all plain sailing, even then. Not by any means." He puffed at his pipe. "Employers are more

4

responsible now, you see: they respect Control of Entry and the Closed Shop. The problem used to be that when they wanted people for small parts in provincial theatres or television they'd just take them off the streets. They don't do that any more. And drama schools are better on the whole now, and more responsible, with smaller classes and higher standards. There's a long way to go there too, though. I'd like to see a more professional approach to drama schools, with employers showing more interest in the training of actors. By interest I mean of course that they should help pay for that training. The BBC pays a fortune on the training of its technicians, but not a penny towards that of the people who are the life-blood of so many of its programmes. I'd like to see drama students being invited to be associate members of Equity, with a subscription of, say, a pound a year, so that they would be more inclined to take an interest in their Union and find out how it works. I would like standards to be more controlled by professionals, and grants from local authorities to students who are accepted by accredited drama schools to be mandatory. It's absurd that grants are still at the whim of different local authorities." He stared moodily at the roof-tops and the sunny weather going on outside.

His face was brown ("My Muswell Hill tan") with a lot of laughter-wrinkles round his eyes: a good public face, photogenic and recognisable for when he has to appear on television. Affable, you would call him, but with plenty of steel inside. A born Trade Union leader, you would say, who has remained loyal to Equity through all its turbulent years and with all its shades of Councils. He has a politician's (or Trade Union leader's) way of speaking, with its careful, syllabic progress through instantly edited sentences, biting away at the consonants, so that "politician" can sound like Polly Titian, the daughter of that well-known painter. "We're lucky to have him," said Hugh Manning, the on-and-off President of Equity. "We don't know how lucky we are."

Anita came back with our coffee and resumed her hectic, electronic typing.

"When actors are on the dole, does Equity have any official

attitude as to whether or not they should apply for Social Security?" I asked, having to concentrate harder all over again.

"Not officially," he replied, sitting down again and picking up his brown cup and saucer, "but if asked I would always advise that should it be needed it should be applied for. Why not? It is their right. They've paid towards it in taxes and National Insurance. Why not?"

"Someone said to me the other day he would never stoop to accepting Social Security."

"An older actor?"

"Yes."

"Yes. A lot of them do find it difficult. They still think of it as a stigma. Younger ones don't any more, partly because so many of them have to apply for it. And it's not just actors: it's white-collar workers and all."

"And what about temporary jobs – Alfred Marks type – does Equity have any connection or liaison with those employers who welcome actors who are out of work?"

"Again, not officially, though we know who they are and they occasionally contact us. The good ones are very good and allow time off for interviews and auditions and things. There are quite a lot who really like actors: many of the big stores, for example, and I don't just mean for their Father Christmasses. They think that actors, with their outgoing personalities, make good salesmen. Pubs too, for the same reason, welcome actors as barmen, and restaurants as waiters. Agencies for domestic work do too: people like to employ actors to clean their flats and houses, because they feel it gives them a certain cachet and they talk about it afterwards to their friends. Companies who need telephone operators for surveys of public opinion and sales promotions are particularly keen to employ actors because of their persuasive and pleasant voices, so much so that they often put advertisements in *The Stage*."

While Peter Plouviez was methodically going through this list of temp. jobs, I was thinking of some of the actors I knew who had had, at some time, to take them. Drab jobs, compared to what they'd had in mind for themselves during their passionate and heady days at drama school. But they're a

6

godsend, really, providing an easy but soul-less way of keeping body and soul together. And it's something to do. There's less time to brood. You can get quite drawn into this strange, new world with its little intrigues and funny things that happen, and as often as not there will be other actors around, so at least you can have the comfort of confirming that there are a lot of others in the same boat, though sometimes you can look round and think, God, and these are only a few of the masses of actors who are out of work! What hope is there! How futile it all is! How demeaning!

But after work you can go off for a drink somewhere and feel low and cynical, and moan to each other, until eventually you get on to the subject of theatre and actors and performances and productions and reminiscences, and somehow manage to chatter about them as though the temp. work never existed.

*

Unfortunately, in addition to the depression a temp. job can induce, there is a deeper snare lurking. Most actors, I believe, have an uncomfortable attitude towards their real work: they love it, otherwise they wouldn't be doing it; but there are dreads as well. There's the dread of not being able to do a part adequately when it comes, and the particularly nasty dread that after the interview or after the audition, when the part is offered, it will prove to be rubbish: you've got to take it, your agent would be furious if you didn't, and beggars can't be choosers. A friend was recently landed with such a part (mercifully quite short) in a dreadful television play. "Oh dear," he said, "I ought to feel elated: I've got a job, I'll earn some money. But I don't. I dread it. It's hopeless. And I'll be hopeless in it. Oh dear." And he panicked.

There's the dread of making a fool of yourself in front of everybody, the dread of being off form when it's important to be on it, the dread of being found out. A most distinguished actress said to her most distinguished director during rehearsals for *Much Ado About Nothing* at Stratford many years ago, "This part is the one in which I am going to be found out to be such a

7

fraud." The actress was Peggy Ashcroft, who proceeded to enjoy great acclaim for her performance as Beatrice.

Most of us have a love-dread attitude to our work. For myself, I love it and dread it in about equal proportions, I think. Sometimes love gets the upper hand and I think, oh good, things are on the up, I'm going to be rather good in this, and then, unaccountably, with the next job, dread does, and I can't fathom out where my talent has sunk to. And the snag about temp. work is that, compared to acting, it can be insidiously attractive. It's dull, yes; it's not what you were put on this earth to do; but it's easy. It doesn't involve your emotions and you're not on show all the time. And all this can take the edge off your enthusiasm to leave no stone unturned to get an acting job. Gradually you can allow yourself to drift out of the main stream and settle for this little eddying backwater, where there is a bit of peace and quiet, and where the turbulence passes you by. I have known several people who dreaded acting more than they loved it, and who opted therefore for the quieter life of the temp. job they found themselves doing. Well, maybe they would have given up anyway: maybe the temp. job merely hastened the change.

Nevertheless, for many dedicated actors who would never dream of abandoning their chosen profession, who live with a vast ambition tucked securely under their skin and an undying hope that one day their turn will come, a temp. job is a necessary part of their working lives, especially if they have a family to keep, or any expensive outgoings, like a mortgage or a car. I suppose the actors who are in the happiest position are those who have, either by their own endeavours or those of their agent, managed to find a niche in sidelines which are connected with acting: radio commercials, and voice-overs for television commercials, commentaries for films, broadcasts (I don't mean to call broadcasting a sideline: it's an important part of the world of drama; but actors who were once members of the BBC rep., and who therefore know and are known by all the directors, often continue with the odd broadcast from time to time), teaching at drama schools, or being the presenter of audio-visuals for internal commercial use. Mostly these jobs

8

require expert use of the voice and mostly they are well paid. Of course, they are so desirable that they are also hard to get, but it's worth persevering. Again, it's just a question of getting started. One thing leads to another.

*

"I wouldn't have your job for all the tea in China," said Peter Plouviez, waking me out of my reverie. He was standing now. It was time for me to go.

"Why not?" I said, getting up and putting on my jacket.

"Because there's no logic in it," he said. "I want a job which befits my merit. If I do that job well I expect promotion; and if I continue to do well I expect further promotion. And so on and so on. With actors it doesn't happen like that at all. People rise and fall with alarming rapidity, often for no discernible reason. And when I see the figures of some people's earnings I am continually amazed: Joe Bloggs, who's had a good year with a few commercials, can earn more than the Prime Minister, while a highly esteemed actor can be below the poverty line."

"Nevertheless there are reputations which, once made, seem to stick and to carry longevity with them," I persisted, "and up to a point one thing leads to another. But I know what you mean. An agent was telling me yesterday about two of his clients. One, a young actor, had the leading role in a television series and was remarkably good in it. But nothing came of it. The other, a young actress, had a bit part in an episode of a half-hour sit-com. The following day the telephone never stopped."

"Typical. Typical," said Peter Plouviez, as we moved out of his office on to the landing. "Of course the trouble is that too many of you are just too bloody good. When standards are high we – by 'we' I mean the public and employers alike – *expect* you to be good. And you make it look so easy. People get used to it. If you were a member of the National Theatre of Uzbekhistan, where the standards are indescribable, people would sit up and take a bit of notice. They would see that good acting is really rather difficult."

9

"The National Theatre of where?" I said, not cottoning on.

"Uzbekhistan."

"Where's that?"

"Oh, somewhere in outer Bengal." He started to laugh.

"How do you spell it?"

"Look. I've told you where it is. You don't expect me to spell it for you as well, do you?" He laughed some more and went back into his office. And I went out into the street, glad of the hour I had spent with this committed, generous and guarded man.

*

And as I walked up Harley Street and across Marylebone Road into Regents Park, on my way home, I thought about what he had told me and remembered how I had felt during a long period of worklessness: ill with depression, brooding endlessly and losing every particle of confidence in myself, not only as an actor. An actor without confidence is nothing. Good acting takes courage and daring.

So the sensible thing is always to be ready; life can change in an instant, at the ring of a telephone: an interview, an audition, or the offer of a part. Out of the blue. It's important to keep up with things – to look good, to sound good, to feel good – and to try to be positive and not bitter, to add constantly to a store of audition speeches, and to keep in trim by doing all sorts of exercises (if possible by attending occasional classes, which have a therapeutic value as well) and by watching and considering other people's acting and your own.

Easier said than done, but . . .

Exercises ⌣

Here are some exercises you might like to choose from. You won't want them all, but you'll know which ones to ignore. Some you can do on your own, while for others you'll need a friend or two.

Stretch Your Voice

Two actors, Colin Blakely and Robert Stephens, were talking to two members of the Moscow Arts Theatre, in London for a season, who had studied under Stanislavski. Naturally they asked them what the great master was like and how intricately he followed the methods described in such detail in his books.

"Oh, he was very practical and encouraged us to be as true and as natural as possible," said one of the Russians, hoping that would be enough; they got asked it a lot.

"What he was really writing in all his books, you see," said the other Russian, taking over, "was an antidote to the heavy, Germanic, melodramatic style of acting prevalent in those days. He wanted a style more suited to the new, gentler, realistic plays of Chekhov and others."

"But of all the things he must have said to you," said Colin Blakely, anxious to know as much as possible, but without wanting to turn the conversation into an interview, "were there any which stand out particularly in your memory?"

"No, no," said the first Russian, disappointingly, "none particularly. He didn't preach much. He assumed we'd read his books, I think. He was good, but no special remark, no."

"Oh come on," said Robert Stephens, "there must have been something . . ."

There was a long pause while they both thought about it. Then from the second Russian came the surprising answer: "Actually, I do remember something he often said, 'The three most important things for an actor are voice, voice and yet again voice.' "

Far be it from me to pontificate on what you should do to improve your voice: there are many experts who have taught and written books on the subject. I have indeed had my share of problems with my own voice; so I thought I would try to remember here what some of them were, and what I did, or was advised to do, to overcome them.

First of all, I think an actor should be able to speak loudly. Easily loudly. Without strain.

"Louder! You should be louder!" said the director Michael Rudman to me, during rehearsals and after early performances of *Donkeys' Years*.

I had spent the previous three years working mostly in television. "But it feels as if I'm shouting," I remonstrated.

"Well you're not," he said, "and you should practise till it doesn't."

And he was right. That's it. An actor with a naturally loud voice can easily quieten it and will still be heard; whereas an actor with a naturally quiet voice will always be full of strain, because it feels wrong when he has to go loud.

I have often been envious of the superb voices of stall-holders who cry their wares in market-places, or the vendors of evening papers who shout at street corners. Hour after hour they do it, sonorously and tirelessly. And I've noticed that when I've been acting in a large theatre for some time, or more especially when I've been on tour, trying to adjust to the varying acoustics of large and not-so-large houses, something happens to my voice, giving it a deeper resonance, a wider capacity. It can go on for longer, at full theatre-pitch, just as those toy cars powered by a certain battery can outlast those using the inferior sort. When I go loud, or shout with full force, it doesn't hurt any more.

And I've regretted that, when I haven't been working in the theatre, I haven't compensated by doing regular exercises, at home, for speaking loudly. I remember being humiliated once in a broadcasting studio when I had to shout in a scene. We did several takes, and afterwards my reddened and unpractised throat hurt unbearably, and I was hoarse, and therefore inadequate, for the rest of the play.

*

Stretch your voice. Half an hour a day, say. A little but often.

Breathe in deeply. Start with a prolonged "h" and gradually, without any hint of a glottal stop, build in some sound, "ah", in your middle register. Increase the volume gently, without any strain, and keep it going for as long as you can. If you get a frog in your throat, cough as gently as you can to release the phlegm and spit it out. Cough only to get rid of the phlegm. Frogs in the throat tend to happen at the beginnings of practice, or at the beginnings of plays. I've often had one in the first scene, never, as far as I can remember, in the last.

Now let your "hah" go up and down the scale: mouth nicely open, plenty of breath, so that you can feel that the tone comes from the chest and passes, without any interruption from the throat, into the room (or remote place in the open countryside!). When a certain volume feels easy, try going a little louder. Then, a week or so later, louder still. What you will hope for is to combine a new capacity for loudness with a tone which is as pure and uncluttered and musical as possible. If you feel there is something really wrong or something you don't like about the tone of your voice it would be worth consulting an expert. Actors with dry, rasping voices, with no liquid notes in them, suffer a disadvantage, I think. We can't all be like Derek Jacobi, Patrick Stewart or Greg Hicks, Peggy Ashcroft, Eileen Atkins or Frances de la Tour (and some may say, well, we don't want to be: we are ourselves, and we want to do things our way); but there they are, they and others, possessors of true theatre-sized, musical, expressive voices. Object-lessons.

You'll soon get tired of "hahing" so you can "mah" for a while. Let the "m" be prolonged until the lips are tingling and then open them gradually into the same "ah" sound.

There are lots of variations of this exercise, using different consonants – L, B, D and K are good ones – and all the vowel sounds. Try to keep the mouth as open for "ay" and "ee" as it is

14

for "ah". Well, the great teacher Clifford Turner used to say that, but it's a bit hard and feels silly, so nearly as open will do. A nice alternative to going up and down a scale is to do off-beat alterations of the note so that it sounds like modern plainsong or a Moslem call to prayer.

Strengthen your voice, and sing. When Mary Martin was appearing on Broadway in *South Pacific* she used to make a point of doing an hour's vocal warm-up in her dressing-room before every performance. She did all the exercises she could think of, and was apparently mortified to learn that her partner Ezio Pinza, the bass-baritone, with his highly developed, magnificent voice, merely said, loudly and slowly, "Carolina" four times before he went on the stage and sang his heart out.

Diction Practice

This is the actor's equivalent to a musician's scales and arpeggios and an athlete's daily slog. There's something of a musician, and of an athlete too, in every actor.

You'll already have your favourites, but here are some more which, if you don't know them already, you might like to add:

*

Go through the consonants from B to Z, including the double ones like Br, Dr, Tr, Thr, Pr, Cl, Shl, Gl, Pl, St, using the vowels

ah ay ee ay ah aw oo aw.

So the first one would be

bah bay bee bay bah baw boo baw.

Etc. Faster and faster.

*

Do tongue-twisters, especially for those consonants you find difficult. An actress who has had trouble with her "s" (it whistles easily) gave me these:

"Six thick thistle-sticks."

"The shrewd shrew sold Sarah seven silver fish slices."

The same actress had to say, in a recent part, "Spanish specials," which was none too easy for her, though it was child's play compared to these four cruel lines:

"Amidst the mist of smoking frosts,
With stoutest wrists and loudest boasts,
He thrusts his fists against the posts
And still insists he sees the ghosts."

Or, an extension of her first one:

"Theophilus Thistler, the thistle-sifter, in sifting a sieve of unsifted thistles, thrust three thousand thistles through the thick of his thumb."

*

Some more consonants, to be practised until they sound easy and uncluttered:

"Betty bought a bit of butter, but she found the butter bitter, so Betty bought a bit of better butter to make the bitter butter better."

" 'Do daring deeds! Do damage!' demanded Dr Doolittle."

"Five flippant Frenchmen fly from France for fashions."

"How has Harry hasted so hurriedly from the hunt?"

"James just jostled Jean gently."

"Keencut cutlery cuts keenest and cleanest of all. Keencut cutlery."

(That was the wording for a television commercial. The actor who did it, years ago, had five seconds in which to get it out. "It was the nastiest session I ever had," he said.)

"Lucy lingered, looking longingly for her lost lap-dog."

"Quickly, quickly, quickly, quickly, quickly, quickly, quickly, quickly."

(To be done quickly; and can you manage it without a whistle,

17

ever, before the "i"?).

"Two toads, totally tired, trying to trot to Tewkesbury."

"Vera valued the valley violets."

*

To strengthen the tongue:

"Red leather, yellow leather,"

and

"Red lorry, yellow lorry,"

over and over again, faster and faster, can hardly be bettered. And what about the "r" sound? To roll or not to roll? It doesn't matter much but it's nice to be able to do both easily.

"Round the rugged rocks the ragged rascal ran,"
and
"Reading and writing are richly rewarding,"
are helpful.

*

For the lips there's obviously, and probably best of all:

"Peter Piper picked a peck of pickled peppers.
If Peter Piper picked a peck of pickled peppers
Where's the peck of pickled peppers that Peter Piper picked?"

But if you want a change, here's

"Pearls, please, pretty Penelope,
Pretty Penelope, pretty Penelope,
Pearls, please, pretty Penelope,
Pretty Penelope Pring.
I would like to buy pearls for Penelope,
Pearls for Penelope, pretty Penelope,

I would like to buy pearls for Penelope,
Pretty Penelope Pring."

or, alternating "t"'s with "p"'s:

"Tippetty-Tippetty was an elfin,
Tippetty-Tippetty, Tippetty-Tee.
Tippetty-Tippetty tripped so neatly,
Tippetty-Tippetty, Tippetty-Tee,
Tippetty-Tee, Tippetty-Tee,
Tippetty-Tippetty, Tippetty-Tee."

*

It is the leaping from the gutteral consonants to those
formed by the lips which can sometimes be so appallingly
difficult. What about

"Peggy Babcock,"

for example?

But you'll know what you find difficult, and practice will
make perfect. Or should. Some obstinacies will cling. After
doing a play for months and months I still found "seriously
neglected" hard to say. Time and time again it would come out
as "serious 'n' glected". And "traditional" can easily become
"trujjnal".

A microphone can point out many things that go silly, like
additional mouth-noises that creep in unawares. When you
open your lips to speak, especially if they are a bit dry, you can
make an involuntary "p" sound. There can be a tongue-crack,
a clatter sound, between the "fierce" and "ly" of "fiercely", for
example, or in any other word ending in "ly". Did it happen to
you when you were saying, "Reading and writing are richly
rewarding"? And your throat can click in the pause after an
"ing" sound, too, so you could be recorded as saying: "Are you
comingk? No, I'm goingk." Just to make this absurd, you might
have a slow go at: "Readingk and writingk are richkly
rewardingk," but if it sounds like that, somethingk is really
wrongk!

19

Nevertheless, the beauty of becoming very practised at tongue-twisters and quick diction exercises is that they will give your speech such precision that when you come to act you will not have to bother about precision. You can forget it, be slovenly, even, if you want to be, if the part calls for it. When a rule or an exactness is mastered, it can be thrown away.

There was a time when, led by Laurence Olivier, actors caught the habit of separating similar consonants which ended one word and began the next. "That day," would never be allowed to sound like "tha' day" (I mean with a silent "t", felt, but not pronounced), or "Yes, Sarah" like "Yessarah". It often presents a problem, this. For example, should our favourite afternoon beverage be described as "Best drink of the day" or "Bes' drink of the day"? I think the unpedantic solution is the better.

*

Finally here's an exercise, very well known, which combines a number of difficulties, and which you could never do too often, because it's such a help. It's from *The Pirates of Penzance*:

> "I am the very pattern of a modern Major-General;
> I've information vegetable, animal, and mineral;
> I know the Kings of England, and I quote the fights historical,
> From Marathon to Waterloo, in order categorical;
> I'm very well acquainted too with matters mathematical,
> I understand equations, both the simple and quadratical,
> About binomial theorem I'm teeming with a lot o' news,
> With many cheerful facts about the square of the hypotenuse.
> I'm very good at integral and differential calculus,
> I know the scientific names of beings animalculous.
> In short, in matters vegetable, animal, and mineral,
> I am the very model of a modern Major-General."

(I was surprised by the word "pattern" in the opening line. I had learnt it, when I was a student at RADA, as "model", and that's how I have said it and heard it from that day to this. But there it is, in an original edition by W. S. Gilbert: "pattern".)

I have proved to myself all over again recently, during a tour of a play, that half an hour spent doing some of these manipulative exercises, either before leaving for the theatre, or in your dressing-room when you arrive, will make all the difference to your performance. When your lips and tongue and voice are ready, your batteries are charged.

Check Your Vowels

It is interesting to hear, when you watch British films made during the war or in the early 'fifties, how pronunciation of so-called Standard English has changed. Some of the sounds they made then have become curiously affected to our ears: their "o"s, as in "coat", were thinner, and their "a"s were much less flat than ours, so that "flat" could sound like "flairt" or even "flet". I was struck by this all over again when I was watching, for the umpteenth time, Celia Johnson and Trevor Howard in *Brief Encounter*.

It's worth checking through your vowels to make sure they are the vowels you really *want* to make. I stress "want" because if you have a regional accent there's no reason why you shouldn't keep what you want of it. It's up to you. After all, it would be dreadful if we all spoke in precisely the same way without any idiosyncrasies, though I suppose you could say that "good speech", whatever its flavour, is required of actors who, along with writers, public speakers and television people, have a responsibility to maintain and maybe, even, occasionally to enhance our language. (So it's good to refer to your dictionary whenever you are in doubt about pronunciation. Controversial words like "controversy", "applicable", "explicable", "transport", "often", "either", are worth getting right.)

Again, it's easy to find or make up your own vowel checks. But here are a couple, for "aw" and the dastardly "oh":

"I ought to call at Dawley Hall
Where my friend Paul, who is not tall,
Has had a fall from off a wall.
His sister Maud has bought a shawl:
I can't afford a shawl at all."

"Golden in the garden, golden in the glen,
Golden, golden, golden September's here again.
Golden in the tree-tops, golden in the sky,
Golden, golden, golden September's going by."

Get Your Sight-Reading Good

Yes, do! It's worth it. We often have to do it. And it comes only with practice. Do it whenever you feel like it, and go on with it until you make no mistakes of either diction or meaning. Go on with it until you feel you are actually *elucidating* the meaning. Go on with it until it feels like talking, not reading: personal and natural.

A rather more boring exercise (because, after all, when you are reading at sight you can read anything that interests you, from a novel to a newspaper, though technical books are a challenge, with their sudden shocks of the names of flowers or diseases) is to prepare a reading, a longish one, as though for *A Book at Bed'ime*, say. Scribble around the words whatever markings you feel you need to help you with the meaning and the phrasing. Among those markings I like to put a little squiggle over bits I know I might fluff on account of having already fluffed them more than once. The squiggle means, watch out, here's a difficult bit, take care over it!

When you've got your reading prepared, go through it three or four times each session, trying never to lose either the meaning or whatever freshness it had when you first read it, but at the same time allowing new nuances to creep in when they occur to you. Try to make it better each time. Go for the words. Go for their meaning. Go for their feeling.

I've put this bit in, about preparing a long reading,

because I find it so difficult myself. My least favourite job is reading a book for cassette or radio. A lot of actors love it but I hate it. The recording sessions seem endless: I can manage the first hour or two, but when they extend for a whole day, as they often can, my concentration withers and I don't know what I'm talking about any more. Shame sets in as the tape is rewound after yet another mistake, and I leave the studio humiliated. If the job lasts for more than one day, as it often can, I arrive the following morning with dread.

I'm still trying to get better at it. But this is more about sustained concentration than reading, and I'll come on to some exercises for that later (having had yet another go through them myself).

What Do You Mean?

For my entire eight years' teaching at RADA I shirked this whole question of *meaning*, and how it was an actor's duty to extract the true meaning from any prose or verse he has to deliver in a way that makes people want to sit up and listen because they know he is being so clear. Harold Innocent once told me he thought the first duty of an actor is to be clear; and that's no bad thing to aim at. When I say I shirked the subject I didn't shirk pronouncing such generalities as those I've just pronounced: I shirked finding examples and setting exercises. I nearly shirked it here because it's such a difficult subject to be clear about.

But last Christmas I had to read the ninth lesson at an annual carol service at St George's, Hanover Square; and the ninth lesson, for which the whole congregation stands, is always that bit from the beginning of St John: "In the beginning was the Word."

"Oh no, not that!" said one of my friends when I told him about it. "That's the impossible one. Nobody ever understands it."

"Consult a priest!" said another. "Try and get him to explain it to you."

Well, I didn't: I decided to try and work it out for myself. But there are problems, as you'll see:

In the beginning was the Word, and the Word was

with God, and the Word was God. All things were made by him; and without him was not any thing made that was made. In him was life; and the life was the light of men. And the light shineth in darkness; and the darkness comprehended it not.

There was a man sent from God, whose name was John. The same came for a witness, to bear witness of the Light, that all men through him might believe. He was not that Light, but was sent to bear witness of that Light. That was the true Light, which lighteth every man that cometh into the world. He was in the world, and the world was made by him, and the world knew him not. He came unto his own, and his own received him not. But as many as received him, to them gave he the power to become the sons of God, even to them that believe on his name: Which were born, not of the blood, nor of the will of the flesh, nor of the will of man, but of God. And the Word was made flesh, and dwelt among us, and we beheld his glory, the glory as of the only begotten of the Father, full of grace and truth.

"Christ," I thought, blasphemously, "what have I let myself in for! I've always thought this bit good but boring; how can I make it good but not boring?" So here it is again with notes about what I attempted. The meanings I ascribe may be thoroughly questionable theologically, but I was concerned primarily with performing it:

In the beginning was the Word (*I tried to find a substitute for the word "Word": something more mystical, like "Idea", "Life Force" or "Space", to make "Word" sound larger*), and the Word was with God (*uniting, in my mind, the two mysteries*), and the Word was God (*they were one and the same*).

(*The next sentence was the hardest of the lot. Is it just an emphatic reiteration of the first? It seems weak and rather boring. Well, I thought, I'll do it emphatically.*)

The same (*i.e., the Word*) was in the beginning with God.

All things were made by him (*big statement*); and without him was not any thing made that was made (*throwing the last three words away slightly, to rid them of any possible absurdity and to make the meaning sweeter. Usually readers choose to emphasise the penultimate word, "was", but eventually I decided that was silly*).

In him was life (*new word, "life"; big word, "life"; felt word*); and the life was the light of men (*their inspiration; another theme introduced*).

And the light shineth in darkness; and the darkness comprehended it not. (*And that was the end of that for now: all the foregoing was ignored, for now.*)

(*New paragraph, new brightness:*) There was a man sent from God, whose name was John. The same came for a witness (*go for the word "witness", and throw the rest away, so it sounds conversational; and wherever "witness" occurs again, emphasise it each time, and do this whole passage about John slightly more quickly than the previous paragraphs, so that the word "witness" ties it all up*), to bear witness of the Light, that all men through him might believe. He was not that Light, but was sent to bear witness of that Light. (*Awkward change to follow: it needs to sound different because suddenly you're talking about Jesus, and that needs to be clear; so let the first three words lead up to the fourth quickly, and then slow down and be as simple as possible:*)

That was the true Light, which lighteth every man that cometh into the world. He was in the world, and the world was made by him (*still very simple, straightforward and true*), and the world knew him not.

(*Putting it another way, but linking it surely with the previous sentence, as though to underline it:*) He came unto his own, and his own received him not (*and throw all the words away except those underlined*).

(*Another awkward transition to follow: so try to make "But as many as received him" sound as near as possible to "However, there were some who did receive him":*) But as many as received him, to them gave he power (*make quite a lot of that word*) to

28

become the sons of God, even (*odd word, "even": it must mean something like "I mean"*) to them that believe on his name: Which were born (*make a nice list here of the "nots" and "nors"*), <u>not</u> of the blood, <u>nor</u> of the will of the flesh, <u>nor</u> of the will of man, but of God.

And the <u>Word</u> (*hark back in your mind to the beginning of the piece – remember the Word?*) was made flesh, and dwelt among us, and we beheld his <u>glory</u> (*make much of that word, and do so again straight away: make a feature of this repetition, just as you did of "witness"*), the <u>glory</u> as of the only begotten of the Father, full of grace and truth. (*I think those last words "grace" and "truth" are so felicitous and deep that they could be separated. "Grace" gets a bit lost if you just say "grace and truth". It could go: "full of grace. And truth." But I don't know. That's what I did, but it's not as simple as "grace and truth" and maybe stands out a bit too much. On the other hand it's a good curtain-line.*)

I found that what I had to do after analysing it like that was try to throw the analysis away, and not exaggerate anything, so that the whole piece would flow in as relaxed and spontaneous a way as possible. The analysis remained, but only just.

*

It will already be clear that the clear way through to the meaning of a piece is not at all by trying to make the most of every word.

There's a spoof of a voice-over session for television commercials. It's called *Blooper's Soap*, was made in America and is very famous in advertising circles. I have a pirated copy of it at home, recorded from a recording which was recorded from a recording *ad infinitum*, I should think, judging by the appalling quality of my little cassette.

The actor arrives, and is given his one end-line, "Blooper's soap is real good", with the instruction from director, "It's just a statement of fact, you know: we want sort of a simple, straight, sincere, throwaway kind of reading." The actor does it perfectly and the director says, "Perfect. I mean what the hell can you do with a simple sincere line? Just say it." The actor enters the recording booth and does a test for level. Then it goes:

RECORDING
ENGINEER: Take one.

ACTOR: Blooper's soap is real good.

DIRECTOR: Sounds fine. Nice easy reading. We'd better take another for our protection, and as long as we're doing it again I was thinking, the Account Executive is a real stickler for client-name identification, so maybe you could goose Blooper a little. OK?

ENGINEER: Take two.

ACTOR: BLOOPER'S soap is real good.

DIRECTOR: I think we got it. Fine, fine . . . er . . . wait a minute. The only thing is our Copy Chief is pretty adamant about product-mention.

ACTOR: You mean soap? I mentioned it.

DIRECTOR: Yes, but not with pride. Mention it with great pride.

ENGINEER: Take three.

ACTOR: BLOOPER'S PRIDE is real good.

DIRECTOR: Perfect. That was it . . . er . . . but you said "Blooper's pride" . . . no, no, it's "Blooper's soap". Have you got a script in there?

ENGINEER: Take four.

ACTOR: BLOOPER'S SOAP is real good.

DIRECTOR: Getting there. Don't lose that nice easy sell . . . could I make one suggestion? The Agency Head is very particular about qualifications. You should hit "real" a bit more, don't you think?

30

ENGINEER:	Take five.
ACTOR:	BLOOPER'S SOAP is REAL good.
DIRECTOR:	That just about wraps it up. I'm satisfied . . . er . . . wait a minute. The Client loved the word "good". He's used it in his copy for years. He's tried to copyright it several times. He spent a fortune, but no soap, you know. Make more out of "good", will you?
ENGINEER:	Take six.
ACTOR:	BLOOPER'S SOAP'S REAL GOOD.
DIRECTOR:	Terrific. But it sounds like "Blooper's soap's real good." You're making a contraction out of "is". Will you give that "is" great conviction?
ENGINEER:	Take seven.
ACTOR (*yelling now*):	BLOOPER'S SOAP IS REAL GOOD.
DIRECTOR:	That's it. We got it. That's just the amount of undersell I wanted.

*

No. The way through to the meaning of a piece is to know what to emphasise and what to throw away. I think the secret is (and I swear I wrote all this before interviewing Prunella Scales) to go for as few words as you can and throw as many as you can away. Then there will be a rhythm to it, a vitality and a life. Let's look at a bit of King Magnus's great speech to his Cabinet in *The Apple Cart*, and see how few words need emphasis:

MAGNUS (*very grave*): The Prime Minister has been good enough to pursue the discussion with me in <u>private</u> to a point at which the issue is now <u>clear</u>. If I do not accept the ultimatum I shall receive <u>your</u> resignations and <u>his</u>; and the country will learn from his explanatory speech in the House of Commons that

31

it is to choose between Cabinet government and monarchical government: an issue on which I frankly say that I should be very sorry to win, as I cannot carry on without the support of a body of ministers whose existence gives the English people a sensation of self-government. Naturally I want to avert a conflict in which success would damage me and failure disable me.

I won't go on; but if the idea appeals to you try the whole speech for yourself. It's a great piece of dramatic prose.

*

Oscar Wilde's plays can be awkward and hard to follow, and unless the acting is splendid the wit can sound stale and the sentiments mawkish. One of the best readings of an awkward line I ever heard (and I heard it a lot because I was in the same production) was by Nora Swinburne in the 1953 revival of *A Woman of No Importance* at the Savoy Theatre. We were coming up to the curtain of Act Two. I was Gerald Arbuthnot and I had just found out that Lord Illingworth (Clive Brook), whom I had hitherto greatly admired, had made advances to my girlfriend, Hester Worsley (Frances Hyland); according to the stage directions I had to be quite beside myself with rage and indignation, uttering the lines:

GERALD: Lord Illingworth, you have insulted the purest thing on God's earth, a thing as pure as my own mother. You have insulted the woman I love most in the world with my own mother. As there is a God in Heaven, I will kill you!

MRS
ARBUTHNOT (*rushing across and catching hold of him*): No! No!
GERALD   (*thrusting her back*): Don't hold me, mother. Don't hold me – I'll kill him.

MRS
ARBUTHNOT: Gerald.
GERALD: Let me go, I say!

32

MRS
ARBUTHNOT: Stop, Gerald, stop! He is your own father!
> (*Gerald clutches his mother's hands and looks into her face. She sinks slowly to the ground in shame. Hester steals towards the door. Lord Illingworth frowns and bites his lip. After a time Gerald raises his mother up, puts his arms round her, and leads her from the room.*)

One can imagine how imperiously Mrs Arbuthnot's last line will have been delivered by the actress in Wilde's own day. Nora Swinburne said it very quickly and urgently, all in one, in spite of herself: she hadn't meant to spill the beans. Then in the pause afterwards, she realised what she had said. And we all looked at her and didn't do any of the other actions suggested in the stage directions. The curtain managed to come down during a rapt silence from the audience, which then broke into considerable applause.

*

No actors are more skilled than John Gielgud and Derek Jacobi at keeping the meaning of a speech rippling clearly along through mazes of clauses and parentheses in very long sentences.

You will see the difficulties involved if you try these three excerpts, which I won't mark up at all: I include them as they are, as fine examples of complicated prose and verse, the like of which you could well be faced with next time you are in a broadcasting studio.

1. The opening paragraph of *The Life and Opinions of Tristram Shandy* by Laurence Sterne:

> I wish either my father or my mother, or indeed both of them, as they were in duty both equally bound to it, had minded what they were about when they begot me; had they duly considered how much depended upon what they were doing; – that not only the production of a rational being was concerned in it, but that possibly the happy formation and temperature of his body, perhaps

33

his genius and the very cast of his mind; and, for aught they knew to the contrary, even the fortunes of his whole house might take their turn from the humours and dispositions which were then uppermost: – Had they duly weighed and considered all this, and proceeded accordingly, – I am verily persuaded I should have made a quite different figure in the world from that in which the reader is likely to see me – Believe me, good folks, this is not so inconsiderable a thing as many of you may think it; – you have all, I dare say, heard of the animal spirits, as how they are transfused from father to son &c., &c. – and a great deal to that purpose: Well, you may take my word that nine parts in ten of a man's sense or his nonsense, his successes and miscarriages in this world depend upon their motions and activity, and the different tracks and trains you put them into, so that when they are once set a-going, whether right or wrong, 'tis not a halfpenny matter; – away they go cluttering like hey-go-mad; and by treading the same steps over and over again, they presently make a road of it, as plain and as smooth as a garden walk, which, when they are once used to, the devil himself shall not be able to drive them off it.

2. From *Eccentric Travellers* by John Keay, the subject here being William Gifford Palgrave, who travelled in the Middle East in 1862, on camel-back:

We were now traversing an immense ocean of loose reddish sand, unlimited to the eye and heaped up in enormous ridges running parallel to each other from north to south, undulation after undulation, each swell two or three hundred feet in height, with slant sides and rounded crests furrowed in every direction by the capricious gales of the desert. In the depths between the traveller finds himself, as it were, imprisoned in a suffocating sand-pit, hemmed in by burning walls on every side; while at other times, labouring up the slope, he overlooks what seems a vast sea of fire, swelling under a heavy monsoon wind, and ruffled by a cross blast into little red-hot waves. Neither shelter nor rest for eye or limb amidst torrents of light and heat poured from above on an answering glare from below.

3. A long single sentence, spoken by Perpetua in Christopher Fry's play *Venus Observed*.

There isn't any reason
Why a sentence, I suppose, once it begins,
Once it has risen to the lips at all
And finds itself happily wandering
Through shady vowels and over consonants
Where ink's been spilt like rivers or like blood
Flowing for the cause of some half-truth
Or a dogma now outmoded, shouldn't go
Endlessly moving in grave periphrasis
And phrase in linking phrase, with commas falling
As airily as lime flowers, intermittently,
Uninterrupting, scarcely troubling
The mild and fragile progress of the sense
Which trills trebling like a pebbled stream
Or lowers towards an oath-intoning ocean
Or with a careless and forgetful music
Looping and threading, turning and entwining,
Flings a babel of bells, a carolling
Of such various vowels the ears can almost feel
The soul of sound when it lay in chaos yearning
For the tongue to be created: such a hymn
If not as lovely, then as interminable,
As restless, and as heartless, as the hymn
Which in the tower of heaven the muted spheres
With every rippling harp and windy horn
Played for incidental harmony
Over the mouldering rafters of the world,
Rafters which seldom care to ring, preferring
The functional death-watch beetle, stark, staccato,
Economical as a knuckle bone,

Strict, correct, but undelighting
Like a cleric jigging in the saturnalia,
The saturnalia we all must keep,
Green-growing and rash with life,
Our milchy, mortal, auroral, jovial,
Harsh, unedifying world,
Where every circle of grass can show a dragon,
And every pool's as populous as Penge,
Where birds, with taffeta flying, scarf the air
On autumn evenings, and a sentence once
Begun goes on and on, there being no reason
To draw any conclusion so long as breath
Shall last, except that breath
Can't last much longer.

*

And now to balance these initial exercises for voice and
speech, here are a few for your body.

Keep In Trim

Again, I wouldn't dream of pontificating on how you should keep in trim, except to say that any time you spend exercising your body to help keep it fit and strong will not be time wasted. An actor requires stamina. An actor needs to be well. He is, after all, someone who is looked at: stared at, even; so you will want to do everything you can to keep your appearance as you would like it to be. Exercise will help. The right food, and not too much of it, and not too many cigarettes will help, too. Of course there are parts for fat actors and if that's what you want, so be it. But it's easy to let yourself go unwittingly, and it's such a waste. And when you're not in trim it can be quite hard to get back, especially as you grow older.

Start From Scratch

All these initial exercises accompany my belief that acting, or rather good acting, is difficult enough without having to bother about a heap of extraneous things which can get in the way of whole-hearted concentration on a part. As I've said, if your speech is right, you don't have to bother about it. Similarly, if your body is right, you don't have to bother about it. Get your everyday self right, and your acting tasks will be halved: I'm such a believer in this that I'm going to dwell on it for some time. Whether you are indeed starting from scratch, or would like a quick overhaul, here are some of the things you can do. Use the mirror if you want to, but when you've got something really right in the mirror, go away from it and do the exercise again without it, so you *feel* the rightness of it rather than merely observe it.

1. Stand. Just stand. Look at yourself standing. Be conscious of relaxing your shoulders, arms and hands. The hands by your sides hang slightly forward, don't they? Stand with your feet slightly apart. Check your stance. Not too wide, not too turned out, just a little. Feet which are too turned out are hard to act on: circular moves become cumbersome, and corners too awkward to turn. Look at your head and neck. Relax them. And make sure your head is level. Neither up nor down. It is very desirable for an actor to have a level head. Turn your head, from side to side, and keep it level.

2. Walk. Go out for a walk. Don't hold anything in your hands and don't put them in your pockets. Let your arm-swing be as natural and as relaxed as possible and keep your head level.

Of course it is nice to hold things in plays, and to put your hands in your pockets, and it is nice to let your head go up and down when you want it to; but it is good to be able to do these simplified stances and walks until you feel comfortable doing them, because they will give you an ease.

If you feel easy in everyday life you will feel easier in plays.

3. Now go back to standing, and investigate, without holding anything, as many different positions of rest as you can think of. There are a lot, and it's worthwhile having as large a vocabulary of them as you can, because they will all come in useful some day. Investigate, particularly, positions for hands which are not identical: not both hands on hips, both hands behind your back, both in pockets, etc. This doesn't mean *never* have identical positions for your hands, but there's a tendency (you will have noticed it in plays) for identical positions to be over-used.

Once you've done this exercise thoroughly, and feel you have plenty of resources, forget it, and even more will occur to you involuntarily. But it's worth doing at some time or other: I recently met an actor who had hardly any resources at all, and it hampered him.

4. Look at your hands. I think a good actor's hand is one which is relaxed and in which all the fingers are visible, equally slightly curved, and slightly separated from each other. This doesn't mean (of course it doesn't) you can't point or clench your fists or strain your hands into peculiar shapes for certain gestures. But it is the hand to fall back on – the basic hand. And the basic gesture is one in which the power travels down the arm towards the hand *getting slightly less as it goes*, so that the hand does not easily become distorted by tension.

Do Everything Separately

You know that one where you pat the top of your head with one hand while doing circular movements round your tummy with the other? Or you pretend to be conducting an orchestra and strictly use the right hand for beating time and the left for expression or bringing in the instruments and not at all for beating time? Well, what follows is an extension of that.

Stand again. As in the previous exercise. And say a known speech. Anything. A nursery rhyme, a speech from a play you've done before, a poem or any of the speeches included here and there in this chapter and which you might like to learn for the specific exercises to which they apply. Stand and speak and do not move about. Do not fidget. Do not *accompany* your speech with anything. "I felt quite proud of myself tonight," said Hannah Gordon, after a performance of *Can You Hear Me at the Back?*, "I managed that whole speech without a single gesture or twitch and with my hands by my sides." And that she felt so triumphant about it, after several months in the play, shows just how difficult it can be. "It felt good," she said.

"It looked good," I said.

Now add one thing. Allow yourself, say, the freedom to gesture with one arm and hand. Be sure that there is no accompaniment from the other. Find helpful gestures for "Jack and Jill", "Little Jack Horner", "Little Miss Muffet" and others. Nursery rhymes are useful for cultivating what I call "echo" gestures, by which I mean gestures which are not a full-force indication of what happens, but a mere echo of it. We use echo gestures a great deal in everyday life, but they can easily get left out of plays. For example:

> Little Jack Horner
> Sat in a corner
> *(Well, if you're going to have any gestures at all you might as well indicate where the corner is. It could be with a full-arm point. But it needn't be. It could be only just indicated. Slackly. And is it a good idea to indicate the corner to your left if you're using your right hand, or to your right if using your left?)*
> Eating his Christmas pie.
> He put in his thumb
> *(See in your mind's eye what he does, then do half of it)*
> And pulled out a plum
> *(This time a quarter)*
> And said, "What a good boy am I!"
> *(Anything at all?)*

Similarly, Jill can tumble downhill with an echo gesture, and Miss Muffet's tuffet is only just small, with a gesture similar to that which might accompany a line like, "Of course I was only so high then."

One more thing to notice, before you go on to the other hand: there is a tendency (especially in beginners) for the majority of gestures to be made with the palm of the hand turned outwards; a whole new range of possibilities can emerge from the hand which is turned the other way: I mean the hand which smoothes a table-cloth.

Now try other gestures, expressive and nicely slack, with the other arm and hand, unaccompanied.

At last use both hands; but for the purposes of this exercise, avoid making identical movements with them. (You don't have to gesture all the time, incidentally! Only when you feel like it and you've got a good one.) What you could experiment with here is putting the main force of a gesture into one of your hands, while letting the other do a similar thing but with half the force, so that it accompanies the first, or is an echo of it. Very useful, this, and very natural.

Now add walking about, and stopping when you want to.

Finally, as the aim of this sequence of exercises has been to get your everyday speech and movement on the right lines and to give you a feeling of easy control, be just a bit aware of what you are doing as you stand and walk about at home and in the street, and talk to people. And watch how other people do it too.

*

PS: Since I wrote these last two exercises I have begun to study the Alexander technique. This has not made me want to alter what I have written here, except to add that the technique explores similar themes with a more fundamental penetration and depth.

Consider Your Qualities

"Oh, I don't know why some people get work while others don't," said Patience Collier to me – years ago, but I've always remembered it. "I suppose it's a mixture of talent, rightness for the part, and niceness. Probably in that order," she added, cautiously.

Niceness. "Oh I do like him," "Oh I always like her": typical remarks from the public. This likeability is an important ingredient in a long career. What is it that makes people like an actor, that gives them that undefined feeling that if they met him they would take to him, no matter how bad-tempered or even evil he may be in a particular performance? Kindliness, or charm, will be at the base of him. If he is charming he will never have to "act" it. He can go far away from it when he needs to. Only those who are not charming have to act it, and usually it doesn't seem to work, quite. It's like a posh voice: when people put it on, there's always something wrong.

Sincerity, warmth and humour are other desirable attributes. If you've got them you won't have to act them. So the greater your stock of qualities, including temperament, softness, sensitivity, ruthlessness, unpredictability and a capacity for rages, the less you have to pretend. Danger has long been regarded as very desirable, the sort of quality which makes stars. "Richard Burton is fascinating," said the director Brian G. Hutton one day while we were working on *Where Eagles Dare*, "because he's so dangerous. You never quite know where you are with him. You're always on your guard. However charming

43

he's being, affable and funny, you know there's something there, dormant now, but waiting to explode."

Brightness is also very desirable. I don't mean just smiling, but a true, inner, energetic feeling, the sort of extrovert brightness all good comedians have. Though to have a nice smile is desirable too. I remember watching, at an Award ceremony, Lee Remick weaving her endless way among the tables to collect hers for Best Actress. Her smile was bright, true and unflinching for the whole of that horrendous journey, and my neighbour Peter Jay, who also won an award, whispered to me, "Americans are very good at that, you know. They work at it more than we do."

I've put all this here, among the Exercises, hoping that you might like to make it one. Remember times past, times when you will have experienced all these feelings. Dredge around for them, search for as many details as you can. Clock your moods and notice yourself.

For Concentration

The places we act in are full of distractions. In the theatre there are people in the wings, walking about and whispering, and in the auditorium there are latecomers and coughs in the wrong place. In film or television studios, or out on location, there are people herded behind the camera, or standing in your eyeline, shifting about restlessly and looking around, clicking stopwatches and checking the lighting. Even in a radio studio the clock ticks loudly; you can hear the Bakerloo Line if you're in the basement of Broadcasting House in London, and you watch, fascinated, as an actor turns the page of his script, oh so very slowly so as not to make a noise, and then at the last moment the paper cracks like a piece of sheet metal and everybody in the control room looks up, startled, wondering if it will mean a re-take. An unheard discussion then takes place and, yes, sure enough, the scene is interrupted: "Go back to speech three on page 46 and, Donald, it's all a bit slow, you know, that's why I'm going back so far, it's *frightfully* slow, so it wasn't just your script noise, Joan, I'd have gone back anyway, but do be careful everybody. All right. Green coming." And you wait for the engineer to re-start the tape and flick the green cue-light.

So an actor has to do everything he can to acquire the knack of being able to concentrate easily in order not to be deflected by all these distractions. Anyway it's much nicer to act when you're concentrating, and really "in it", rather than merely observing what you are doing from somewhere outside yourself. And that, truly, is the difference that concentration makes.

Here are some exercises:

1. Try to think of anything you would like to think about for five consecutive minutes, undeflected, unhindered. Think through an argument, organise your reasons for your belief in something, go through details of a memory or of jobs to be done: something like that.

Make it easy for yourself, to start with, by doing this at home, alone, and with your eyes closed. Later, make it more difficult. Try it when you are in a bus or a train, or when you are walking down a street.

2. The important thing is to be able to concentrate *at will*. We can all concentrate when the mood takes us. For example, after you have been to see a really gripping film and you come out into the street afterwards, you know you have the mood of concentration. You know that the people you pass in the street (those who ignore you and those whose eyes you catch), the lighted shop windows, the traffic lights, the cars and buses and taxis swishing by, all have a heightened dramatic significance and you are part of the drama. It is tempting, no, it is delicious, when you get back home, to open your wardrobe door and look at yourself in a full-length mirror, and act out some tremendous scene. You are very dramatic, and full of meaning and intent. You are very talented. Was there, really, ever any doubt? If only people could see you now!

There is some conjunction, then, between concentration and talent. What you were doing was concentrating. What you felt was talent.

Notice and examine this mood when next you have it. It won't spoil it. It will teach you a lot.

3. Can you generate this after-cinema mood at will? It's hard. But try this:

Think: "Let my thoughts go back from my eyes. Instead of projecting them forwards, out of me, let me keep them inside my

46

head. Let them go back. Back to the back of my skull. My head contains my thoughts. They go back, back, back to the back of my head . . ."

Try it, easily, hypnotically, for a few minutes at a time.

4. At your party, play Kim's game. A tray is put in front of everyone for about three minutes with thirty to forty small articles (a pin, a penny, a nail file, etc.) on it. After it has been taken away, lists must be written of what was on it. He who remembers most wins. But subtract a mark for anything listed which was not on the tray.

5. Another game to make your party swing! You all sit round and the first player says "I went to market and I bought a bar of toilet soap." The second player says, "I went to market and I bought a bar of toilet soap and a second-hand vacuum-cleaner." The third: "I went to market and I bought a bar of toilet soap, a second-hand vacuum-cleaner and a pound of cooking apples." And so on, round and round.

Notice the desperate devices you use to cling to your memory: the association of one article with another, consecutive articles which begin with the same consonant, or, more importantly, the association of the article with the person who thought of it. In the game I've just started here, you might think, ah yes, Joan always wants to be clean, ah, so does John, but round the house and, ah, in the house Marilyn likes to cook pork.

I once played this game with a class of twenty students, at the excellent City Lit. in Stukeley Street, as a rather frivolous end to a three-day seminar, and we managed to go round six times before everybody started to collapse. Not bad though: 120 articles, remembered in the right order!

6. And if your friends will still stay with you for another, more serious, exercise, you might like to try this one. I first saw it done in a television programme a long time ago, in which the late Harold Lang, a talented and volatile teacher, was taking a class of Central School students. They sat round in a semi-

circle and, to a student at one end of it, Harold Lang handed a piece of screwed-up paper. The paper had to be passed from one student to the next until it reached the end of the line; each time it represented some specific object: a mouse with a broken leg, a valuable small painting, a sparrow, a piece of very fragile glass. The purpose of the exercise was to point out the sort of concentration that objects command; and I remember Harold Lang being particularly emphatic about the difference between true, straight, unaffected concentration on the *object* and a self-indulgent concentration on their personal *reaction* to it. One student, in advance of receiving the paper the first time round, had obviously thought, I know, I'll act being squeamish about mice, and when it came to his turn his face was a model of distaste and displeasure. He was concentrating so hard on his face that he gave no thought to how he was actually handling the mouse, which, from his ridiculous grasp, would have escaped, or been dropped. The *task*, after all, was to receive a mouse and hand it on. The *mouse* had to be concentrated on, not the emotional reaction to it.

7. To follow from that, observe how you use objects in everyday life. Notice in particular the difference between the attention you pay to objects you know well and to those you don't know at all, like staircases, paintings, streets, ovens and kitchen utensils.

Oh yes, there's a lot you can do in everyday life. But when it's done, it's done. Habits will be formed, and it won't be such an effort any more.

For Listening

Two simple exercises: one for practising listening, the other for observing it. Both are best done with a group of people.

1. Get someone to tell you a long tale: a personal reminiscence, or an event they witnessed, or the story of a film they have recently seen. After the tale is ended, you must relate as much as you can remember. Re-arrange the facts if you like. It's good to do this. Clarify them. But include them all. Add any observations you made about the story-teller's attitudes to the subject. The story-teller and the others will mark you out of ten.

Good listening, like everything else, is habit-forming. "I don't like her very much because she never listens," said one actress about another. She was talking about her behaviour off-stage, not on: but she didn't listen on, either. It was the word "never", unstressed though it was, which was so indicting.

2. Recently I met two people who listened perfectly. One was a detective, the other a solicitor. Of course it is their job to listen; but what an object-lesson they both were! I met the detective in the company of other actors (he was giving advice about an investigation scene) and after he'd left us we exclaimed, severally, "Did you notice how he answered Tony's long list of questions in the right order? Point one, he said, point two, and so on. He'd just stored them up." "Did you notice how still he was?" "Yes, he didn't move his legs at all when he was sitting over there in the corner watching the scene. He didn't

cross or uncross them or anything." "Yes, and his face was still, too, and gave nothing away. Only his eyes moved. He just . . . well . . . he just listened." "And watched." Unforgettable, that afternoon's rehearsal.

And I thought again, when I was talking to the solicitor, privately this time, and watching him listening to me, that because there was so much energy going on in his head, there was none left for any fidgets or reactions. You can see the same thing on television when a politician receives complicated questions from an acute interviewer. You can see him storing them up, icily assessing them and sifting them and working out his necessarily edited replies.

The following exercise for observing listening adds one more ingredient: that of transferring attention from one person to another. So place two people, who will be the talkers, in chairs on either side of the room, and add the third, who will be the listener, between them, the arrangement to be something like this:

⊓ the listener's chair

⊏ the talkers' chairs **⊐**

Ask the talkers to discuss any topic they mutually agree to. Ask the listener to listen and not to participate at all, but warn him that you will be asking him questions about the content of the discussion afterwards.

Watch the listener. How relaxed is his posture? How absorbed is he? If he is absorbed, how do you know? How does he transfer his attention from one to the other? Does he always look at each, full in the eye? Does he turn on cue? Or is there a delay? Does he know, instinctively, which of the two speakers is the protagonist at any given moment? If he does, does he ignore, at any rate physically, questions thrown in from the other? But if a question is an elaborate one, does he turn to the other in advance, waiting for the reply?

Of course, the listener here is in an extreme position: up-stage centre. But if the listening has been good, you might have found he helped you, in the audience, to follow the discussion, instead of distracting from it, by guiding your attention to the most important place.

For Talking

This is my favourite exercise with which to start a class, or seminar, or workshop or whatever it's called, at the Actors' Centre or wherever, because everyone learns a lot from it and it's such a good ice-breaker. It has the advantage of being as exciting for the onlookers as it is for the participants: it is like looking at life through a microscope.

I ask someone to volunteer to tell as personal a story as they will to one other member of the group, both sitting, the listener downstage of the talker. Particularly vivid in my memory are the story one girl told of what it was like giving birth, and details from another of the day she moved house and all the awkwardnesses involved. One boy told of an exhausting journey on a Greek ferry from Kos to Patmos and another described how, when he was a boy, he and a friend tired of throwing darts at a dartboard, so decided to throw them at each other, until one lodged itself firmly in the middle of his forehead.

There is no time limit. But after it is over I will ask the class if they think that, had it been learnt and acted instead of improvised, they would have judged it good. Or not.

"Oh yes, good," chorused the class, after the girl's story of the birth of her baby.

"Why?" I asked.

"Well, because you could *see* it all. It was so vivid."

"Why was it so vivid?"

"Well, because she was seeing it all herself. You knew it was true."

"She was backing everything with pictures in her mind, was she?"

"She must have been. It was as if the words just floated out, because of what she saw and everything she'd gone through."

"So you felt, did you, there was more going on inside her head than showed?"

"Oh yes."

"More mental energy than physical?"

"Oh yes."

"Yes. Anything else you noticed?"

"She laughed a lot. I mean it was a sad story, really, and painful too, but she smiled and laughed a surprising amount."

"More, you think, than she would probably have done had it been a speech from a play?"

"Oh yes."

"Yes. But it enhanced the sadness of the story, didn't it, that she didn't give in to it all the time?"

"Oh yes."

"We laugh more in everyday life than we tend to in plays. Anything else? Did you think she was telling the story to that particular listener?"

"I did," answered the listener, quickly.

"But she didn't look at you all the time, did she?"

"Oh no, but that was because she was so full of her story."

"Anything else? What about her movements?"

"Her gestures? Well, they were all so natural."

"Of course. They *were* natural. But in what way?"

"Well, they weren't too much. They seemed to accompany what was going on in her head. I mean when she said the baby was tiny she didn't sort of measure the baby, but she did a little, vague, movement bringing her hands slightly closer to each other."

"Yes. The gestures were an echo of what was going on in her mind. Not an accurate description. Like when she said she'd had to traipse through the snow; she just did a to-ing and fro-ing with her shoulders, and you could feel the trudging, tiring steps."

"Yes, and what I liked was the way she sometimes corrected herself."

"Yes," laughed the class, remembering.

"I mean, when she said, 'I was twenty-three, oh no, I wasn't, I was twenty-four, just, it was just after my birthday,' it was wonderful: she did it so quickly, and threw it away, and laughed."

"Did you think, if that had been in a play, it would have been sufficiently entertaining? One would possibly have been tempted to put some moves in, I suppose, and there would have been no harm in that."

"No, in fact I nearly got up once but then I thought no, he said sit," said the girl.

The class laughed again.

"But even as it was, would it have been entertaining enough?"

"Oh yes."

"Why?"

"Because it was so true."

*

That was the first girl. Then the second got up. For her the task was slightly different because she knew what we would be looking for. Would this make her self-conscious? Curiously, it didn't seem to. Nor, curiously, does it ever. Occasionally I ask the volunteer to leave the room before telling their story, and ask the class to look for something specific which the performer will not know about, like the varying rhythms of speech, or the times when they look their listener full in the eye, or the revelations of their personality and attitudes yielded by the story and the way they tell it.

Try this exercise for yourself. Tell your stories to real or imaginary people. Place them in chairs so you know where they are.

All this is easy enough to do, because you know what you are talking about and have vivid pictures in your mind. In everyday life the thoughts come first, the words follow. In plays, because they have to be written down, the words come first. We

54

have to work backwards, therefore, to support them with thoughts and pictures.

Try one or two of the following three speeches. Learn them and perform them, and see what happens as you get to know them really well and supply them with more and more background. No characterisation is needed. It's just you, talking to someone.

1. We sat there for ages at the top of the Downs. It was evening, and very still, and we looked out over the low-lying fields. We couldn't quite see the sea. We'd had a nice day, had lunch with some friends in a pub called . . . oh . . . er . . . I think it was called the Fox and Plough. I don't know. Doesn't sound right. It was nice. Beautiful garden, terribly hot today so we sat on a terrace which had a sort of translucent roof-thing over it. Sarah was very funny, telling us stories about Noël Coward, how he never liked to be seen, even by his closest friends, until he was bathed and shaved and groomed and dressed. Or half-dressed, trousers and shirt and tie and then a dressing-gown. I was glad of today, because I'd been feeling low . . . don't know why . . . just sort of vaguely miserable. Well, not so vaguely, perhaps. But . . . low. Yes. Funny. Anyway. We just sat there, amazed at the view. It got quite chilly, because it was about seven o'clock and the sun was getting low. But we'd had a good day. I think Jo enjoyed it too.

2. We spent Christmas that year at a small hotel in Buxton. It seemed convenient because I was working at Sheffield and only had Christmas day off. We were doing our usual musical play for children and had given a performance on Christmas Eve and had two on Boxing Day. Anyway father came over for me and we drove to Buxton quite quickly, through Baslow, I think, and Bakewell. It was a very dark night, and we had to keep dipping the lights as cars passed. It was quite warm in the car and I'd got my presents all wrapped up in a box I'd got

55

from the local greengrocers in Sheffield. It was on the back seat, and I occasionally looked round to see if it was all right. It was about . . . oh, well after midnight when we arrived. Mother and sister had gone to bed and father was tired so he went up straight away. I stayed up a little while, talking to the owners, I've forgotten their name now, er . . . oh, it'll come to me. We had a drink, said Happy Christmas, and I was shown my room. I crept about so as not to waken anybody. I had a single bed which was against a wall, and there was a washbasin in the far corner by the window. I undressed quickly, had a wash and cleaned my teeth, and went to sleep. The following morning I was wakened by a tapping, quite loud, on the wall by my bed. "Wake up," I heard my mother say. "Time to get up. It's eight o'clock." Some more tapping. "Are you awake?" So I tapped back, said, "OK, OK," and the tapping stopped. I looked at my watch and it was just after eight so I got up rather grumpily, I could have done with another hour, and went down for breakfast. "Why did you wake me up?" I said to my mother. "I didn't," she said. "You did. I heard you. You said it was eight o'clock and it was." "It wasn't me," she said. "Was it you?" I said, turning to my sister. "No," she said. "Anyway," said my mother, "it couldn't have been any of us because we're on a different floor. We're on the second, and you're on the third." "How odd," I said. And after breakfast I went upstairs to have a look at the room next to mine. It was locked, and it didn't have a number on the door. And when I asked the owner he said, "Oh we never use that room, it's always locked. We keep our junk in there." I never got to the bottom of it, but I know I hadn't dreamt it . . .

3. After the funeral everybody came home. It was a relief to drive back at normal speed instead of that ritual slowness which made the journey there seem endless. Pointless, really, just done for tradition's sake. Holding up the traffic because they're not supposed to pass, and

everybody in the street stopping to stare. Why point it out to everybody, I thought. But, as I said, the journey back was better, and there were about thirty people, and we'd worked all morning cutting up the meats, and making the salads, and doing the bread and butter and covering it with a wet handkerchief so it wouldn't go dry. We'd got quite a lot of drink in and people could have what they liked. We were a solemn lot as we traipsed into the house, and people said things like, "Oh it's very sad, isn't it?" and "We shall miss him, you know." But I felt a curious kind of elation. He'd been so terribly ill and he didn't want any more of it and had said so and, well, I don't know, I was a bit mixed up, really. But I wasn't . . . downcast or anything like that and anyway, here we were, having a party. So all we could do was make the party go. Well, the drink went straight to Aunt Renie's head and she became very jolly, talking about her family and what they'd all been up to, and this seemed to catch on, this jollity, and everybody said how nice the food was and we really shouldn't have gone to all this trouble; and when we were all sitting round having coffee and talking in little groups, Auntie Nellie, who comes from Halifax, suddenly said rather loudly so everybody stopped talking and listened to her, "Oh, you know, I shouldn't say this, but it's been a really good do. It's been really enjoyable. And I think your father would have liked that." And everybody went quiet, thinking about him for a little while.

You could make up similar stories of your own. If you do, try to recall the experience in as great detail as possible. Don't try to feel, merely recall the detail. If you've got a recorder and a microphone you could tell a story into it, learn it and perform it, keeping the tape as a guide as to how it originally sounded when it was fresh and spontaneous, because freshness and spontaneity are of course what this exercise is all about.

Pay Attention

Two speeches now, to concentrate your attention not so much on the substance of what you are saying as on whom you are saying it to.

You are addressing two people, Peter and Paul. They are on either side of you, downstage of you. Choose good moments for looking at Peter, good ones for Paul, and good ones for using the space between them. Easy enough, obvious really, to find them in Speech A, where the direction of each thought is implied by the sentences. Speech A tells you how to do the exercise. Speech B is less clear, but should be as clearly marked by you as the first.

A. Yes, Peter, yes. I *think* so. What do you think, Paul? Do you think Peter's right? I'm in two minds about it, really. On the one hand I see your point, Peter, but on the other I'm not sure. Oh Paul, come on, you must have an opinion. I wish I knew what to do. What shall I do? Paul?

B. I know what I'll do: I'll go and see someone else . . . someone I knew a long time ago. He should be able to help. Funny, isn't it, when you *need* help it doesn't seem to be forthcoming? Well, one day anyway. One day it'll all be sorted out. Yes, I'll go and see Patrick, I think. Do you remember him? It's . . . oh . . . five years since I've seen him. He lives in Wandsworth now.

Try the same exercise (talking to more than one person, more than two if you like, and using the spaces between them), with other speeches that you know, or perhaps with the speeches in the previous exercise.

Divide Your Attention

Now, use those same speeches to practise dividing your attention between talking to someone and doing something else at the same time, like:

sharpening a pencil,
making yourself up,
polishing shoes,
washing up,
knitting,
eating,
drinking,
reading a newspaper,
going for a walk,
driving a car,
being a passenger in a car, looking at the view,
looking out of a window,
looking out of a window, waiting for someone.

I like this exercise because it tells you so much. It tells you the places in the speech where you must give it your whole attention and stop doing the other task (except driving, of course!) for a moment. It tells you the peaks, therefore. It sways the speech, gives it its ups and downs.

But when you are doing it, remember that the other task must be done. It is important to get that pencil sharpened. And sharpened properly: if the content of your speech is full of

60

passionate emotion, beware of taking it out on the pencil, otherwise you'll break the lead. I once saw an actor taking it out on a pair of shoes he was supposed to be polishing: he was getting very worked up about something, and because the brush and the shoes were getting equally worked up, you knew that the shoes weren't being polished properly. They were just smothered in the stuff. So it all looked ridiculous.

What's Your Continuity?

"Continuity" is the connection of things: one minute with the next, one day with the next. It is an underlying mood, induced by the sort of person you have become and the circumstances you find yourself in. If, for example, things have become very bad for you, your continuity will be one of depression; but that does not mean that everything you do within that continuity is necessarily depressed. A cup of tea can taste nicer than on a happy day, an affectionate word can be more welcome, a joke more of a release. The fact that you are depressed makes certain things better.

It's like the sea. The continuity is the water underneath. The water underneath and the surface are of course one and the same thing but they appear to be different and have different qualities. There could be no surface without the water underneath. And the underneath is vast and changes only slowly. The surface is smooth or choppy and always changing. It is the surface which is pelted by the rain, warmed by the sun, whipped up by the wind; it is on the surface, too, that traffic moves.

Or, really, it's more like a river. There is the water underneath and there is the surface. It is the surface which is cut through by the ships (the people who cut through you); it is the surface which is influenced by the weather (all those external things which influence you), which sparkles in the sunshine and which is darkened by the shadows of bridges (your minor ups and downs). But a river is going somewhere, and the water underneath and the water on the surface travel together, widening and deepening as they go.

*

It is essential to find the flow of your continuity through a part. It is what unifies it, binds it together, prevents it from being a mere assemblage of bits and pieces. "How could she laugh like *that* when she's feeling like *that*?" we can often ask of someone's jerky performance. It isn't that she laughed which we query, it is the way she laughed, which seemed unconnected with what had happened previously.

In a poorly written play, one without depth or imagination, or with a poorly written part, one which is nothing more than a pawn in the author's story-telling game, you will have to invent your own continuity in order to give it any life at all.

Refer again to the three speeches at the end of the exercise For Talking. Try doing them with different continuities. In speech 1, how low are you? Why? Low enough not to snap out of it despite a good day? Or happy enough to have forgotten the temporary low spirits, finding them now hard to imagine, like a cold when you're better.

In speech 2 how dismissive are you of the mysteries of the tapping on the wall? Or has it remained an intriguing reminder of your belief that "there are more things in heaven and earth . . ."?

In speech 3 you can choose between various underlying moods: dislike of the rituals of cortèges and funerals, sadness at the loss of a parent in spite of laughs at the party, or relief that the painful days of a terminal illness are over and surely it's better now to celebrate the life than to mourn the death.

For Relationships

Use the same speeches, or any others that you know (and knowing them is important: you will get far less from these exercises if you just read them), and do them as though you are speaking to

> your little child,
> your teenage son,
> your best friend,
> someone to whom you are newly attracted,
> your lover,
> your family,
> your boss,
> a stranger.

For Intentions

What do you intend to achieve by what you are doing? Try the same speeches with the following intentions:

to entertain your guests at a dinner party;

to make someone, whom you suspect doesn't like you, sympathise with you;

to have the last word with someone: you've got to go, you're in a hurry, and this must be the end of the conversation;

to recall the events for a psychiatrist, in the hopes that it will clarify for him your attitudes and opinions;

to talk frankly to someone you hardly know in the hopes that they will be prepared to reveal more about themselves;

to make conversation, trying to get your mind off something which is really worrying you: to cheer yourself up;

to convince a detective, who has accused you of being somewhere else on that particular day, that you were not lying;

to cheer up someone dear to you who is very ill in hospital.

Use Your Imagination

This exercise is not as frivolous, nor in some cases as easy to do, as it may look.

Mary had a little lamb
Whose fleece was white as snow,
And everywhere that Mary went
The lamb was sure to go.

It followed her to school one day,
Which was against the rule:
It made the children laugh and play
To see the lamb at school.

Try this nursery rhyme in the following ways:

as if you can't quite remember it: you have only just learnt it;

as if you are making conversation to a stranger, in any place, while waiting for someone else to turn up;

as a sermon about Mary and Jesus;

as cocktail-party chat;

as cocktail-party chat when some piece of your clothing – a belt, braces, a suspender belt – has broken;

as cocktail-party chat: a very full cocktail-party, this, so you have to stand close to people and shout;

as if you've got the giggles about something else (like you do in plays);

as if you are drunk;

as part of an electioneering address by a junior education minister;

as if talking to someone you love, but you haven't told them yet;

as a voice-over for a television commercial for wool;

as if to a foreigner with very little knowledge of English;

as if to tell a young girl why she can't take *her* pet animal to school;

as if you are the director of a film to be called *Mary*, telling the story to an actor up for the small part of the headmaster;

as if, in the course of an interview for a part you badly want, you are telling the director the story of the last film you were in;

as if talking to someone who is wearing a toupee for the first time and you're determined not to look at it;

as if you are a guide showing people round an art gallery; you are describing a picture of Mary and her lamb at school; you've had the job for five years and it's the end of a gruelling day;

as if you are a Sunday-school teacher taking the toddlers' class;

as if the lamb has just died;

as if Mary has just died;

as if you are a television newscaster reading an obituary about Mary, using an auto-cue.

Improvisation

The classes I used to take in improvisation at RADA were some of the most exciting the students and I ever experienced, and when the two participants became really involved in the story the rest of us would sit riveted, wondering what they would do and how it was going to turn out and what emotions would be forthcoming. We watched them with penetrating eyes, and afterwards discussed details of the feelings, the actions and the development of the story, with the relish of knowing we had observed, therefore, in the heat of it all, discovered new facets of human behaviour.

It had been Anne Kimbell, an American actress who had studied under Lee Strasberg at the Actors' Studio in New York, who told me how to set an improvisation. "Arrange it so that the actors start at the moment of inevitable clash," she said, while we were having tea at Valoti's in Shaftesbury Avenue, after a matinee of *Roar Like a Dove*, which we were both in. "So limit it to just two people. It works better. It's less complicated. Tell them a long story of their past lives, leading them nearer and nearer to the moment of crisis. Give them enough specific facts to build on, so they don't have to invent any. I mean it makes an improvisation impossible if, for example, one partner in a marriage says to the other, 'You know that time when you got out a knife and threatened me with it?' and the other is taken totally by surprise because it wasn't included in the lead-up story. The whole point of choosing a peak moment of clash is that it will then be a question of will against will, and nothing at

68

all to do with making up dialogue. A bad improvisation would be one which was set like this: 'So you're waiting outside this movie-house, see, and your girl-friend is late and you look at your watch and think, hell, is she coming or isn't she, and then you notice this girl, also waiting, also impatient, so you go over to her and talk. OK? Let's see what happens.' All they would have to do is to talk, to make up dialogue or, if they've any sense at all, to say, 'I know, there's a coffee-shop over there, let's go and have a coffee,' and exit. Anyway, the winner would be the one who could talk the best. And that's not fair. And it's not what it's about.

"So. A few 'don'ts', Peter. Don't set a time limit: let them go on until the situation is resolved or there's a stalemate. Don't let them characterise, because that gets in the way: they start concentrating on it. And don't, as I say, let them invent anything about their past lives. That means your story will have to supply them with a lot of facts, and last for some time. This will establish a mood, too, in the classroom. Don't rush anything, but be sure that when you leave off they've got to solve the problem, right now."

Here's an abbreviated version of one of the stories I evolved. I tried to include in all of them experiences with which drama students could easily identify: some of them were therefore perilously close to home. I'll call the couple here John and Diana.

*

To John I would say, "You are you," and to Diana, "You are you. With these differences:"

To John: "You were born of rich parents, who live in Alderley Edge, a smart outer suburb of Manchester where your father was and still is the Chairman and Managing Director of a successful business, manufacturing medicines and drugs. The firm has been in the family for generations and has never ceased growing. You were brought up in the lovely Cheshire country-side, attended a local prep. school and eventually went to Rugby. You were an only child and have always been rather pampered. Your favourite toy had been a model theatre, and

69

you acted quite a lot at school and once with a local dramatic society where you were pronounced 'good'. So with no other particular talent rising you thought you might as well have a go at being an actor. You'd heard it provided a fairly easy life once you got started, and you knew you had a nice voice and a pleasant appearance. You'd also heard it was an attractive profession socially, especially at a drama school where there were bound to be a lot of pretty girls. Your parents did not object openly to your idea: in fact your mother was quite pleased and enjoyed telling her friends that her son was going to be an actor. So on the strength of your good voice and appearance, and with the aid of plenty of coaching, you got into RADA. Once there, you just managed to get by: you were not highly regarded vocationally, but socially and sexually you were as successful as you had anticipated. You were a popular boy."

To Diana: "Your parents were less well-off and you have a younger brother, Jonathan, who also wants to be an actor but who, so far, after many attempts, has failed to get into a drama school. He is beginning to feel he must be hopeless and may well soon opt for a course at a technical college so that he can teach English, which is his next favourite subject. If he does so he will be following in your father's footsteps, as he is the senior English master at the comprehensive school at Enfield which you attended. You were very successful there, being clever at nearly everything without having to work too hard: this was because you found most of the subjects, from maths. to athletics, so interesting that it took the slog out of it all. You converted enjoyment into success. You were the leading light of the dramatic society and when, each year, it produced the set 'O'-level Shakespeare, you were Viola, Portia and, eventually, Lady Macbeth. You knew, as everybody knew, that you were going to be an actress. You auditioned for RADA and got in."

To both: "I can tell you this summary of your lives before you met because obviously you will have told each other. You met at RADA, you were in the same class, you found each other attractive but did not have an immediate affair: your friendship grew slowly and deepened slowly; and only eventually did you realise you were very much in love. You married while you were still there, in your final term. You, Diana, moved into John's flat, which was adequate (the rent being paid by his father) and in the University area of Bloomsbury. You were idyllically happy. As far as your careers at RADA were concerned yours, John, was unremarkable, but yours, Diana, went from strength to strength: you won several prizes and at the annual competition, attended by casting directors, agents and others, you were snapped up by a top agent, Julian Belfrage, of Leading Artists Ltd, and you immediately landed a leading role in a television series, starring Ian Holm and Denholm Elliott, called *The Well*. Your photograph appeared on the cover of the *Radio Times* with your two co-stars and you scored a major personal success when the series was shown.

"You, John, got nothing from the same competition. No agent seemed interested: and when you rang round you were unable to speak to any of them personally. Secretaries intervened. You wrote letters and got some replies, the most encouraging being from the casting director of Granada Television who said he would bear you in mind whenever he was casting a new play or series. As yet, though, there was no work, and Diana was out all day rehearsing or recording, and sometimes staying away for days on end, filming the outside sequences for *The Well* in Hampshire. You looked after the flat, did the shopping, cooked the meals and washed up.

"From *The Well* you received several offers, Diana, and you asked John for his advice. You always got him to read any scripts which arrived and growingly you relied on his judgment. You agreed that the most attractive of the immediate offers was a sequence of four separate two-hour plays for television in the *Thriller* series for London Weekend. This also involved a considerable amount of filming away from home, and very long hours.

"You were still happy together and glad of the albeit curtailed times when you were both at home. Work for you, John, remained hard to get, although you did have a tiny part in one episode of a Granada series called *Tales of Hadrian's Wall*. Happily your time away, when you lived at home at Alderley Edge, coincided with Diana's filming for *Thriller*.

"You both realised that the conventional husband-and-wife roles were being reversed. Diana was the bread-winner, out all day, obsessed with work, delighting in it, but getting tougher in the process. You said to him one evening, 'I don't want to get hard but, really, if you don't stand up for yourself people ride rough-shod over you: I mean, if it's a bad line I ask for it to be changed, and if I don't like a move I say so.' Your confidence was growing and you received a lot of praise.

"Your confidence, John, was withering, and you surprised yourself one evening by confessing to Diana that if you got a part now you'd be terrified of being inadequate in it. 'I think I must be hopeless,' you said, 'otherwise people would want me . . .'

"After *Thriller*, Diana, you had a film-test for a starring role in *Dark Angels*, which was to be Michael Caine's new picture. This was about a year ago. You got the part. Nothing, you felt, could stop you now. The flat in Bloomsbury was suddenly no longer adequate and together, before the film started, you looked for somewhere else to live and found a pleasant, unpretentious house with a large garden in Weybridge. A mortgage was easily forthcoming on the strength of Diana's earnings, and you both enjoyed choosing curtains and carpets and furnishings, and arranging it all. You had a very happy two months together, undisturbed by work, though sometimes, when John started in the garden or did an extra job in the kitchen, you Diana, would disappear upstairs, to do some learning. And when the telephone rang, as it often did, it was nearly always for you.

"Filming started. First of all there were six weeks in the south of France, followed by four months at Pinewood for which you had to be up at six o'clock most mornings, arriving back at around seven-thirty most evenings. John always had dinner ready for you. You acquired a daily woman, who comes three mornings a week, and, at your instigation, John, a dog, a Yorkshire terrier called Hunter. You take him for walks every day.

"Diana was beginning to think that a certain amount of entertaining was now a necessary accompaniment to her work, so friends from the studio were occasionally brought back for dinner. Prepared, of course, by John.

"After *Dark Angels*, which finished shooting about four months ago, there was a lull in Diana's work. But there were invitations to First Nights, film premieres, and lunches at grand hotels. These gave you, John, no pleasure at all and you said so; but you insisted, Diana, that they were important, very good for publicity and, as you said to him, 'Who knows, something good may well come of it all for you? And, anyway, it's fun.'

"Your new film is called *The Bright Day* and for the first time you have top billing. Your co-star is your old friend Ian Holm. Just before production starts you have a serious talk one night about children, and you make it quite clear, Diana, that now is the wrong time to start a family. You could not afford the time off required for the pregnancy, and you would not have the time, either, to look after a young child as a mother should. 'We can afford a nanny,' said John, 'and I can do a lot of the looking after that has to be done.'

" 'But what happens if you get a job?' said Diana. 'And anyway I don't want to have a nanny looking after my child.'

"*The Bright Day* started shooting six weeks ago and Diana's routine is again a gruelling one.

"A week ago a letter arrived for you, John, from your father. He said he wanted to talk to you and asked that you visit them for a few days."

*

At this point I ask John to leave the room so that I can talk to Diana alone.

"When John is away, and you wonder what his visit up north is all about, you realise that you still love him a great deal. You are surprised how much you miss him. He has become your home. And for you the arrangement is perfect. You wish he were happier and had more work but at least he is no competition for you and his softness and your ambition go well together in your eyes. You are regarded as a happy couple enjoying a happy marriage and you know that this is good for your career. You would acknowledge, if pressed, that sometimes his diffidence and reticence in public irritate you, but you do everything you can to hide that. You would acknowledge, if pressed further, that your rapid success carries strain somewhere within it and that you are not necessarily happier or easier to live with because of it. Are you becoming hard? Are you becoming selfish? No, you cry convincingly, not selfish, not at all: after all, I'm paying for him. You have been tempted, from time to time, to sleep with other men, especially when filming away from home, but have so far resisted the temptation. It is a growing possibility that you will yield to it one day; John is wonderful to you in many ways, but he is not exciting any more and grows less so in your eyes.

"While he is away you are sent a play to read. It is called *First and Foremost*, it is by Simon Gray, the part is excellent, though one of a team, and an impressive list of names for the cast is being approached by the director Harold Pinter. It would do you good, you know; your first love is still the theatre. A six-week pre-London tour is envisaged and, from your reading of the play, it should be an enormous success when it arrives in the West End. Julian Belfrage has told you that you will have a good salary but that you will have to agree to a nine-month run in London. You are very tempted indeed, especially as it will give you, once it has opened, far more time at home. This is good news. You can't wait to tell John about it and get him to read it and ask his opinion. Michael Codron, who is putting it on, has already telephoned to ask what your reaction is. You stalled, saying you hadn't quite finished reading it yet. It's obvious he's anxious for a quick reply."

Then I ask Diana to leave the room and send John in.

"You are very dissatisfied, John. You're not exactly jealous but you hate the role you have come to play, that of the one who looks after the house and garden, who does most of the shopping and is always in the background. Even the move to Weybridge has not helped: in fact it's made matters worse because it's taken you farther away from your old RADA mates and any other friends you made while you were there. You are lonely, and feel out of it all; the people who come to your house are her friends and not yours. You still love her, though she is not as sweet and loving as she used to be. Her obsession with her career is making her hard, in your view, and self-sufficient. You do not see how the marriage can last. You want children and you need to be the master. You suspect she has been unfaithful to you, especially when she went to the south of France, but the subject has never come up and you have no proof at all.

"You tell your mother and father quite a bit about all this. Your father, in return, tells you he is retiring in a year: he asked you to come home to discuss the possibility of your taking over the firm. It would involve spending the coming year preparing for it by studying each department from the chemists' to the accountants'. The job would carry a large salary, to be agreed, which would be increased generously from time to time and which would enable you to live at least as well as in Weybridge. You would of course have to move to the Manchester area, choosing, no doubt, one of the smarter outer suburbs. Not necessarily Alderley Edge.

"It all seems exactly what you want. You already have a considerable knowledge of and interest in pharmaceutics, on account of hearing so much about them when you were a boy. You have always known secretly that your father was a little disappointed when you opted for the stage, while he and your mother have known for sometime that you are unhappy about the lack of work. For Diana, well, it would be a very hard decision for her to agree to move up north. Her career would be more awkward to organise, might even become well-nigh impossible. But this could carry many advantages: you could raise a family, she would become something of a legend, and she would, you are sure of it, revert to her old self again, because you are equally sure that if she persists in her career she will harden beyond endurance, grow less happy rather than more, and probably become promiscuous. And you couldn't bear that. You have remained utterly faithful to her throughout your married years. She may well regard the whole idea as an impossibly dreary alternative to her present mode of living, but you are sure that with the extra care and attention and love you would give her she would not find it nearly as dull as she may expect. And it needn't be the end of her career. She could work from time to time. But your present role-playing is impossible,

75

your attitude to it will deteriorate rather than improve, and you would like to be the breadwinner.

"Your father has said he would like an answer very soon. In fact he has said, 'When you've talked it over with Diana, ring me.' The train journey back to Euston and on to Weybridge seems endless."

*

Diana comes back into the room. The time of day is established (Diana home first from the studios, John back at, say, eight-thirty p.m.) and the two of them plan the room together: which room it is, where the doors are, what furniture there is, what it looks like. Are there any drinks? Newspapers? Books? What lights are on, and is there a telephone? It's better to have props than to mime, but the important thing is to agree what there is.

Then, with a final reminder that there is no time limit and a reiterated warning against inventing any further details of the past, John leaves the room to give Diana a minute or two to be alone at home. When he is ready he returns and the improvisation begins.

For those who perform, it is an unforgettable experience; for those who watch, an engrossing, even educating, play.

Telephone Conversations

This and the next two exercises are again for two people and it is probably best to start by improvising them. However, you will not reap the benefit they can give unless you then write down what you say, or at any rate consolidate the words in your minds so that you can repeat them exactly, as you would in a play. Do not characterise: just be yourselves, and make the conversations as trivial as you like.

So, for this one: improvise, then write and learn, the two sides of a telephone conversation. Include in it:

talking at the same time as each other,
interrupting each other,
laughing at something the other person has said,
being distracted by someone else or something in the room you are in.

Perform the entire conversation together, if possible using two prop telephones.

Then perform the two sides separately. What adjustments do you have to make so that your part of the conversation is *entertaining* enough on its own? Certainly you will want to speed up what the other person says, because he has now become a silence. But not too much. Do you want to make your listening more active? Perhaps a little. But not too much.

This is one of my favourite exercises because you learn, merely by doing it, all you need to know about telephone conversations. They're easy. It's such a pity they are so often done badly.

Getting About

Improvise, write and learn your own scene to incorporate a lot of moves hither and thither. The kitchen, with all its activities, is a nice room for this, although it could be more general housework or preparing a room for a party or anything like that. Use as many objects as you can and, by turning your attention as early as you can from one thing to the next, do the scene as quickly as possible. Make a rule: no pauses!

I won't write a whole scene, because you will want one to fit where you are and what you've got and what you want to do. But here's a brief example of the sort of thing I mean:

> (*It's her kitchen. He is the visitor. She is cutting some bread.*)
>
> SHE: Darling, you lay the table will you? The knives and forks are there (*she goes slightly towards where they are*), the mats are over there (*ditto*), and you'll find the salt and pepper in that cupboard (*she starts to return to the bread, while he gets the knives and forks*). Hell, the bacon needs turning (*she goes to the oven*).
>
> HE: I'll do it (*he makes for the oven*).
>
> SHE: No no, it's all right. I can manage. What are you doing there?
>
> HE: Looking for the salt and pepper.
>
> SHE: No, it's not that cupboard, it's that one.
>
> HE: Oh sorry. Look, the eggs are sticking. I'll do that.
>
> SHE: All right, thanks. Kitchen utensils in that drawer.

It's good to be nimble when you've got to be, and get those feet going round the room.

Standing Around

Improvise, write, learn and perform a duologue for standing around, the way people do. Circle round each other a bit, as people do when they talk at street corners. Take it outside, and do it at a street corner! Or on a walk. Or in a queue. Or in a room. Don't hold anything and don't hide your hands.

Bad Habits

This is a check-list of the more common bad habits. They are only bad, incidentally, if they are indeed habits and you do them, therefore, too much or too often. The best remedy is to acknowledge the habit and refuse to allow yourself to indulge in it *at all* for some time, until you realise how much better you are without it. So here's the list, with some suggestions for exercises:

Fidgeting.	Go through, right through, the exercises called Start From Scratch, and Do Everything Separately.

*

Perpetual use of restricted gestures: cramped, and from the elbows only.	Say "I open my arms like a cross." During "I open my arms," raise both arms, parallel and forwards, fully extended, to shoulder-height: and during "like a cross," open them fully sideways, like a cross, still at shoulder-height.

*

Repeating the same gesture too often, especially if it isn't a good one anyway.	Enlarge your vocabulary of gestures.

81

*

Fading out at the ends of sentences, or fading in at the beginnings.

Say any nursery rhyme so that each line is consistently loud from its first to its last word, but change the volume for each new line:

"(*very loud*) Mary had a little lamb (*whisper*) Whose fleece was white as snow, (*medium loud*) And everywhere that Mary went
(*quietly*) The lamb was sure to go."

*

Going blank at the ends of sentences.

Again use a nursery rhyme, but this time put enormous pauses between each line, and carry the thought, and therefore the expression, of the line you have just uttered, right through the pause.

"Mary had a little lamb (*pause, pause, pause, think of the lamb, think of the lamb, think of the lamb, pause, pause*)
Whose fleece was white as snow (*pause, pause, think of the snow, think of the fleece, pause, pause, pause*) . . ."
And so on.

*

Being too regularly intense, which is often accompanied by being too wide-eyed.

Relax in a chair or sofa, as you might on a psychiatrist's couch, and do known speeches,

82

perhaps from the part you are now studying, as though dreaming them, through half-closed eyes, without ever looking at the person addressed. Talk to him, as it were, through the ceiling.

*

Blinking.

*

Wrinkling the forehead too much.

*

Using nods of the head for emphasis.

*

Joining the first word of the next sentence to the end of the present sentence, pausing, and repeating it: "I went home. I . . . I didn't feel very well. I . . . I wanted to lie down; and . . . and have a good cry. So . . . So when I got home I went upstairs. And . . . And I lay on my bed and . . . and cried."

*

Repeating the first words of a sentence: "But but I don't understand you."
"After after I'd done that . . ."

Stopping at all the full stops.

*

Running sentences into each other too glibly.

*

Coming in on cue too glibly.

Listen, right up to the final consonant. Remember: you have to pretend you've never heard it before.

*

Dipping your eyes on the turn from one character to another, especially on the stage when they are on either side of you.

Do the Pay Attention exercise and keep your eyes up as you turn between Peter and Paul.

*

Being unable to take inflections.

Everyone knows that giving inflections is rather frowned upon nowadays, but directors often have to have recourse to it, as it's a quick way of getting results. When a radio play has to be recorded in a day, or a commercial in fifteen minutes, there's precious little time for lengthy reasonings. It is dreadfully shaming, on such occasions, if you can neither hear nor repeat an inflection, and you'll just have to work at it. And it isn't nearly so bad a way of directing as some people think: it is shorthand, after all, and avoids tedious explanations which are often more harming than helpful.

*

Talking to the audience instead of to the other characters.

*

Being a ham.

*

Being a hack.

Never, never say, "Well, as long as they pay me . . ."

Special Skills

If you've got any, you might as well make the most of them, as you never know when they will come in useful and indeed be a contributing reason for getting a job.

The Spotlight now sends us all an *Artist's Accomplishments Form* with a daunting list of little boxes to tick if you can do, and do well, what it says. Foreign languages and accents, dialects, types of dancing, singing, sports ("please insert ONLY if you are of above average ability") and Special Skills ("e.g. Flying, Juggling, Mime and any other unusual qualifications of high standard").

I would add, as very desirable skills, on which the landing of a part can often depend: horse-riding, driving, swimming and all sorts of fighting. Never say you can do something when you can't, and come clean straight away if you see that a part requires, say, that you drive a car and you're a non-driver (if the director really wants you he'll be able to accommodate your inability, but if you don't tell him in advance so that he can plan what to do about it, he'll just be cross); and be sure that, if you claim to be able to do a regional accent, it is an accurate one, belonging to a place or a county, and not just vaguely Scottish, north country, or posh.

Have Party Pieces Ready

Eric Portman said, "Any actor worth his salt will have some party pieces ready." We are entertainers, after all, and are often asked to get up and do something, either at a house party or at a charity function. It's nicer to be able to say yes than no. It's easier.

So why not search for and learn one or two? It's a change from searching for and learning audition speeches, which I'll come on to now.

Auditions ～

When someone comes on to a stage or into a room, you notice first of all what they look like, then what they sound like, and then you wonder if they are any good or not.

There are two kinds of auditions: those at which you will be asked to perform speeches you have learnt and those at which you are asked to read for a particular part.

*

You will certainly need audition speeches if you want to get into a drama school or a permanent repertory company; but any director casting a play or film might well ask you to show him a piece or two you have prepared.

I think the thing is to keep increasing your stock of pieces whenever you can so that you can pick and choose, and not always have to do the same old thing which can so easily go off and get stale; and when you are choosing your pieces to be sure to cast yourself well. Use them to show the director what you are like. Let one contrast well with another, but don't attempt to be versatile, unless you think versatility is your strong point. Variety, not versatility.

The best audition speeches are those which are self-sufficient, needing little preamble, avoiding, therefore, this sort of introduction: "Well, you see, the thing is this character has just come back from a party, which she didn't enjoy very much, and when she got home she was surprised to find a note waiting for her, and in this note it said a friend of hers was very ill and would she go round as soon as possible, but then there was a knock on the door, and it was the woman from the upstairs flat who was in a desperate state so this character just had to spend some time with her, all the while knowing that her friend was waiting for her . . .''

No. A self-sufficient speech. A memory. A story. Everyone loves a story. It doesn't have to be amusing, but it's no bad thing to get a laugh or two. It doesn't *have* to be from a play. It can be a poem, a piece of narrative from a novel or from the Bible, or a speech of your own which you've composed and learnt.

If it is from a play, know the play and not just the speech. Know where it comes in the play and what the story is at that point.

Here is a most arbitrary list of plays which contain ideal audition material:

> *Make and Break* by Michael Frayn,
> *Duet for One* by Tom Kempinski,
> *Season's Greetings* by Alan Ayckbourn,
> *Way Upstream* by Alan Ayckbourn,
> *The Dresser* by Ronald Harwood,
> *Night and Day* by Tom Stoppard,
> *The Real Thing* by Tom Stoppard,
> *Travesties* by Tom Stoppard,
> *The Deep Blue Sea* by Terence Rattigan,
> *The Beastly Beatitudes of Balthazar B* by J. P. Donleavy,
> *Tonight at 8.30* by Noël Coward,
> *Dear Octopus* by Dodie Smith,
> *After the Rain* by John Bowen,
> *Not Quite Jerusalem* by Paul Kember,
> *A Man for All Seasons* by Robert Bolt,
> *Murder in the Cathedral* by T. S. Eliot,
> *Can You Hear Me at the Back?* by Brian Clark,
> *The Caretaker* by Harold Pinter,
> *The Homecoming* by Harold Pinter,
> *Strindberg* by Colin Wilson,
> *Plenty* by David Hare,
> *A Map of the World* by David Hare,

Teeth 'n' Smiles by David Hare,
Equus by Peter Shaffer,
The Royal Hunt of the Sun by Peter Shaffer,
The Public Eye by Peter Shaffer,
Bent by Martin Sherman,

and most of the plays by Christopher Hampton, Peter Nichols, Joe Orton, John Osborne, Arnold Wesker and Simon Gray. Then of course there are the classic authors: Shakespeare (nice things in the less frequently performed comedies), Shaw (*The Apple Cart* has a lot to offer), Chekhov (*The Seagull, Uncle Vanya* and *The Bear* are happy hunting grounds), and the great Americans if you want to do an accent: Tennessee Williams, Edward Albee and Arthur Miller.

I'm sure I've left myself open to charges beginning, "But what about . . . ?" and "Fancy including . . . !" But the plays are those I happen to have read or seen, and the authors are those I admire.

*

When someone comes on to a stage or into a room, you notice first of all what they look like, then what they sound like, and then you wonder if they are any good or not.

So when you've chosen your audition speech, prepare it properly. The director will suss out fairly soon whether you've worked on it or not and will deduce from that whether you work hard or not in general. Direct it well, or have someone direct it for you. Put some moves in, whatever it is. If you don't, the director will wonder why, and suspect it's because you are not very good at moving about. Recently I saw an audition speech done by someone who I was told afterwards was extremely talented, but I'd thought he probably wasn't because he'd done the whole thing in a monotone and had sat slumped, in profile, all the time. Well, this might have been all right if it had been part of a performance of the entire play, and it's nice to know that actors *can* sit still and be slumped in profile and talk in a monotone. But an audition speech is a vehicle for showing what you can do, and it will help the director if he hears something of the range of your voice and sees your body in different positions. And it's in an audition speech that you really ought to upstage any other characters so that the director can see your face.

The presentation of your pieces is as important as the choice of them, and I'm amazed that so many people will risk mugging something up at the last minute and trotting it out without care or work. Believe me, it shows. There is no point in being seen unless you are seen to your advantage.

Beware of relying too much on props. or on arranging furniture, as this is time-consuming and boring, though certainly you can put a chair or two and a table, which ought always to be there, where you want them to be, preferably at the same time as announcing what the piece is. In short, get on with it; and have alternative productions in your mind in case of lack of furniture or space. A young actor told me that he now tries to choose pieces which are as apt as possible for the place he finds himself in: he had sunk with embarrassment, apparently, shouting a big, declamatory piece of Shakespeare in a tiny room. This is another advantage of having several things up your sleeve: some best for a stage in a large theatre, others for a pokey little room.

*

When someone comes on to a stage or into a room, you notice first of all what they look like, then what they sound like, and then you wonder if they are any good or not.

Many a director nowadays chooses not to ask you to do prepared speeches, but relies instead on interviewing you. He may, or he may not, ask you to read something from the part he is considering you for. Try not to object, in your mind, to the form of audition he chooses: it really is up to him. He may well have heard in advance of your reputation – he will have asked around – and will therefore want to see you only to have a look at you and to hear you speak, to see if you match in any way his conception of the part. He will be weighing you up with the other people he is considering for the other parts, to see if you will coalesce. He will also be wondering if you are likely to be a good company-member, if you are easy to get on with and unlikely to cause trouble. If he asks you to read a scene with him, he may give you some notes and ask you to read it again. He will be watching to see how you respond to his direction.

So it's good to go for an interview in as good a mood as possible; and in a good talking-mood too, having done some talking, to yourself or to others, before you go; and in a good listening-mood. Really listen to what he says. It's so easy to half-listen when you're nervous. If you give your full attention to what he says it will help alleviate your nerves and you'll be able to have a proper conversation: you will be revealing yourself more than you think, and without trying too hard.

Try not to have rules about whether or not you should have a sight of the script beforehand if you have to read from it (remembering that a little knowledge can be a dangerous thing); and if you know in advance what the part is, don't go dressed exactly as you think you ought to look, because that will smell of trying too hard and relying too much on the clothes. M'm, clever, the director might think, not necessarily admiringly. On the other hand, as a well-known director said, if the part is that of a nun, it's silly to go with an exotic hair-do and a skirt with a split up the sides. Go with some sort of approximation to the look of the part, but only some.

In his book *Conversations with Ayckbourn*, Ian Watson quotes the Director of the Stephen Joseph Theatre at Scarborough thus:

> Robin Herford (my Associate Director) and I go to endless trouble when we audition.
>
> I'm talking about actors particularly, and of course they are the most delicate. What you cannot tell is how an actor will socialise. You look and hope he isn't a heavy drinker; and you check with a few people, and you look at the references, but ultimately you employ him because you like the look of him and because he looks as if he can act. I have little faith in auditions, and I loathe those big workshop sessions that go on for days. It's an awful thing to say, but I tend to like people when they walk in the door. And, of course, this occasionally leads to disasters;

we've had some extremely inferior actors in the company from time to time; we've had actors who've drunk; and we've had some that have been so anti-social and so unpleasant that people longed to get rid of them, because you are in fact asking people to live in each other's pockets for twelve hours a day, and in a very small concern of eight, nine actors with a communal men's, communal women's dressing room. So it's tricky, and obviously we make mistakes. You can't hope they'll all love each other: what you can hope is that you can gather people together who, although they may well see each other's errors, respect each other as artists.

*

They are a nuisance, are auditions. But they are here, and they are here to stay. Some are well run; some are hideous: crowded, rushed, demeaning. "If this is the way they do it, I'm not sure I want the job anyway," one is tempted to say. All one asks for is a little time, a little courtesy and a little attention.

A friend told me recently of an audition he had attended at The Warehouse in Earlham Street. After the appointment had been made, he was sent a speech from a play the company was about to produce, together with a note that it was to be read and not learned by heart. He was asked to have one speech of his own choice ready, and was also supplied, to his great surprise, with copious information about the company: its aims and its fields of activity.

He arrived at the agreed time. The director came out to the waiting area and said, "I'm extremely sorry, but we are running a little late. Why don't you go for a coffee somewhere and come back in about fifteen minutes?" During the audition the director was attentive, encouraging and thorough. "I'd like you to read our speech again," he said. "At least you've solved it, which most people haven't managed to do because it's so difficult. Very good. The only thing is, the emotional pitch you achieved at the end is really how you should have started it. So do you mind doing it again, starting more or less where you left off and rising from there? Very good, though." And he muttered encouraging remarks while the rising was attempted. Afterwards he said that if there were a recall it would be within three days. In fact, my friend did not get the part. But the director rang him at home two days after the audition to tell him so, to thank him for the trouble he'd taken and to say, again, how impressed he had been.

The company was the Actors' Touring Company. If only all auditions were held like that!

Nevertheless, the idea is of course, to get the job; it can be very dispiriting when you don't, especially if you've put a lot of hope into it. I've tried to console myself when I've failed an audition by saying, "Well he obviously didn't think I was the best for the part so it's just as well I haven't got it: rehearsals would have been awkward and I'd have sensed his displeasure and lost confidence, so I'm probably well out of it."

But it doesn't really work. At least not for long.

Attitudes ⌐

I realise I've got thus far without having yet found an answer to that question put to me in the Hayward Gallery: "It's all very well if you've got work, but it doesn't tell you anything about how to get it, does it?" I was reminded of this all over again the other day, when a girl said to me, "I just wish someone would write a book telling an out-of-work actress how to get a job."

Well, Clive Swift's book, *The Job of Acting*, is full of advice about letters and contacts and agents and auditions and photographs and all the paraphernalia we need to try to sell ourselves to prospective employers.

But I have noticed that there are many actors and actresses, far more than I had supposed, who, for some incomprehensible reason, do not do their best when they *get* a job, and who therefore *ensure* that their present employer will not want to work with them again. "I could never recommend him to anybody," said a company manager to me about a lazy, unreliable, undisciplined and boring actor who wasn't much fun off-stage either.

So this is going to be a very po-faced little chapter indeed, all about good behaviour and trying hard. Why throw away what opportunities you get?

There are obvious things like always being early and never being late for rehearsals or performances. Take your work seriously; but don't talk about your performance unless you have to, don't brag, don't bitch unless you've absolutely got to, and don't take up a disproportionate amount of the director's time. Look as if you're enjoying it even when you are not, and be nice and kind and funny and helpful, and if you've got a good idea, say it. And try not to judge the others too much.

*

Yes. Try not to judge the others too much. It's so easy to have double standards: to be mercilessly critical in your heart about the others, when all the time you are making excuses for your own lapses and lacks. It's so easy to think like this:

"Of course today is the day of the read-through and of course one is not expected to give a performance at the first reading. Actually, someone said to me once that he thought people who give good first readings are extremely suspect, and will probably go off as rehearsals proceed; they are probably facile, I remember he said. So although I know my reading must sound flat and boring, and as though I've done no work on it at all, which is *not* true, everyone will know that it is just the first reading and not to be taken too much notice of."

Or: "Of course this is the day when we are given moves by the director, and everyone will know that that is what I'm concentrating on, and not on the acting, though he has irritated me several times by saying how such and such a speech should go, but really, first things first, let's get the moves done and *then* concentrate on the acting. Left to myself I'll be able to work on my speeches, thank you very much. I made it quite clear, albeit *very* subtly, that I was trying to concentrate on the moves which, my God, are very odd and absolutely no help at all."

Or: "Of course this is the day when we do it without books for the first time, and everyone will know just how awkward such a day can be. I don't really know it yet, I'm struggling for the words, and I'm making it quite clear that I am struggling by drying more than I need to. And another difficulty is that whereas I've always had the book to hold before, today I haven't. And I don't *quite* know yet what to do with my hands. Or where to look. I always had the book to look at before. That's why I'm either staring the other actors out or looking at the floor."

96

Or: "Of course the trouble is my part is just not well written. In fact I think it's the worst part in the play. In all fairness to the author I have to say I didn't think so at first; but first impressions are necessarily superficial: and since then I've tried to plumb the depths only to find there aren't any. There's no real character there, and there are impossible switches of mood. And the actual words I have to speak, well I mean I try to think of alternatives but I can't because the author's words stick, good or bad. Mostly bad. Anyway I'll have to tell people I'm finding it awkward because then they'll know what a problem I've got trying to be good in this awful part."

Or: "Of course everyone will know that the reason why my performance is not as good as it ought to be is that the director is so hopeless. I mean he's all right with some of the others and I agree with what he says about Brenda Browning because she's so dreadful; but as far as I'm concerned he doesn't understand me. He doesn't understand what I need at any given time; he doesn't understand the phases that I go through: for instance, I'm feeling my way gradually into this appalling character and he doesn't help me at all with his little picky notes. What I need, and he should know this, is gentle guidance and encouragement. I'll have to have a word with some of the others, especially those who I can see are also worried, so that they know exactly what I'm up against."

Or: "Of course everyone will know that Dafydd Dryden is an appalling actor and just impossible to act with, and unfortunately all my best scenes are with him. He gives nothing and he doesn't listen either, and the reason why our scenes fall so flat is that he is no bloody good."

Or: "Of course it's the dress rehearsal and I have to say I'm completely thrown. The furniture is not at all where the stage management put it in the rehearsal room, and how they expect us to act on that sofa I really don't know: I mean you just sink down and disappear in it. And it's impossible to get up out of it. We had hard wooden chairs at rehearsal and no one warned us it would be like this. Also my clothes don't fit properly and the pockets are not where I asked them to be. Anyone who is fool enough to go out front and watch will know how completely thrown I am."

Or: "Of course now it's the First Night and I'm really desperately nervous."

Or: "Of course we're on tour now and this theatre is VAST compared to the one last week. It's hopeless to be expected to adjust without a proper rehearsal. Anyway, everyone will know that the reason why I'm shouting is that I haven't quite got the measure of it yet."

Or: "Of course I've been playing this play for far too long. I try to keep it fresh but it's an uphill struggle. But everyone will know and make allowances."

But they won't, will they?

*

Oh, we do have extraordinary attitudes towards each other sometimes. A Very Famous American actor, who has ambitions to be called great as well as famous, confessed of his ambivalent feelings towards the people he was acting with. On the one hand he wanted to be the best, and therefore feared that if anyone else was too good they would constitute a threat to his supremacy; on the other hand he knew he ought to be surrounded by splendid performers because the product would be better and more likely to be successful, and he would shine all the more.

I suspect we've all got a bit of that in us. I know I have. It's very odd. Why do we so easily think we are in a competition instead of a play?

*

To restore a proper perspective, and to keep our attitudes clear, it would be no bad thing to ask ourselves from time to time, "Why should there be plays? What good do they do? What's so special about them, that we devote our lives to performing them? Is there anything they give to audiences which couldn't be obtained from books, newspapers, music, the visual arts, lectures, after-dinner speeches, conversation, church services, documentaries, talks, sit-coms, *Call My Bluff*, *Round Britain Quiz*, *This Is Your Life*, or *Desert Island Discs*?"

Although we would all acknowledge there is a lot of overlap

98

between the pleasures from plays and those from all the other things, the answer must be "yes", and "yes" several times over. You will have your own favourite "yesses". One of mine is: "yes", because of the laughs. Eight hundred people in a theatre roaring away at the stories, dilemmas and jokes (not just jokes, as from a variety performer, but stories and dilemmas too) supplied so freely by Alan Ayckbourn, Tom Stoppard, Michael Frayn and the other funny ones, are sharing a delightful experience made all the more delightful because it is shared. Laughter is catching, and they laugh more loudly and more often than they could possibly have done had they seen it on their own; and this intensification, this enlargement of their reactions makes a play memorable and life-enhancing. Any serious content pierces more powerfully because it has been cloaked in laughter.

And "yes", because when a play is so momentous that it becomes an event, drawing the audience into its world, into the story and characters, suspending disbelief as far as disbelief can ever be suspended – as happened in recent years at *Nicholas Nickleby* at the Aldwych, *Peter Pan* at the Barbican, *Duet for One* at the Duke of York's, *All My Sons* at Wyndham's and *The Rivals*, *Lorenzaccio* and *Translations* at the National – when the audience responds without reserve to the immediacy and presence of what is happening on the stage, there can be no feeling like it in the world.

My favourite "yes", however, comes from television. In all programmes, other than plays, the performers are putting on a public face. They are aware of the camera and, through the camera, of the millions of viewers they are addressing. News-readers have a public face: composed, dignified, a slight smile for good news, a warning seriousness for bad. Panel-game players grin to the camera as they say, "Good-evening," and laugh more glamorously than they would bother to at home. Variety performers – well, they really do have a public face: nothing can cloud their jollity, their enveloping smiles, their manic energy. Even people being interviewed or appearing in a documentary know that they are being photographed and are altered because of it. A friend of mine, Mischa Scorer, who makes documentary films for television, said to me, "The trouble is that the presence of the camera changes what is happening: you would like to photograph those kids as they *really* arrive at school, as they *really* behave in in the classroom, as they *really* play up to the teacher; you would like to photograph that Arab at his vegetable stall in Cairo as he really is, but you can't. You have altered him: he is self-conscious and he puts on a public face."

Plays are the one area left for privateness. Actors are the only people who have to pretend that there is no camera there. This does, I think, give them a particular responsibility: they are there to show the private face, to show what it's like to be that sort of person, what it's like to be angry, selfish, generous, in love, ecstatic, depressed, lonely, excited, exhausted, ill – whatever the play demands. They are there to show what life, with all its suffering and all its joy, is really like, so that the audience can say, "Yes, that is it . . . yes, I recognise that . . . yes, that is what it's like." That is the stuff of drama; that is why there should be plays

How Do You Work On A Part?~

The idea for this chapter came from a conversation with Gerald Harper, who said, "What I'd like to get from a book about acting is something about how to work. I still don't really know how to work on a part or how to rehearse it. And I certainly don't know how other people work or rehearse."

Oh, I thought afterwards. Right then. I'll ask.

Judi Dench

I asked Judi Dench, who is married to Michael Williams, on Friday 21 January, 1983. She was then appearing in two plays in the repertory of the National Theatre: *The Importance of Being Earnest* by Oscar Wilde and *A Kind of Alaska* by Harold Pinter.

*

JD   The bit I like most about acting is when I'm asked to play a part, because I don't like rehearsing it and I don't like doing it and I'm sad when it's over. That's a joke in a way, but in a way it's related to a tremendous truth. When I've been offered a part I feel as if I'm standing on a great hill. I never read up about it: I mean I barely read the play. I prefer, as in the case of *The Promise* and *The Wolf*, which Frank Hauser directed, that he should come for supper and, while I'm preparing it and we're having a glass of wine, he tells me the story of the play in my kitchen. I like being told the story in somebody else's words.

I'll tell you what I know now, as certainly as I know I'm sitting in this mustardy chair. I know that if, for example, I have to get up impossibly early for filming, I can wake at the required time, have my bath and get dressed to go. In the same way, if I'm giving a dinner party, there's something in me, not fabricated, not imagined in any way at all; like a bell which I actually hear go off and which I know means it's the moment when I've got to go down and start cooking so that I can finish exactly at the moment I need to. If ever this goes awry it's because something unforeseen has happened like a telephone call which goes on for a long time or I've smashed a plate or something like that, but it's never because I've started late, because I always have this person inside. I also do the crossword, the *Telegraph*, and in the morning I look at the crossword but I don't fill any in, and I can think, yes I know that, yes, yes, yes. I'll read the rest and then I'll put the crossword down. And in the evening, when I come back, I can fill in over half, because this person who wakes me up at the required time has also been doing the crossword during the day.

Now once I've heard the story of the play, if it appeals to this person who's inside me I think, oh yes, I'll do that. Of course it's got a lot to do with the director.

Having been offered the part – you don't mind my going on like this do you? I'm feeling quite lucid this morning, more lucid than usual.

PB Please . . .

JD Having been offered the part I just feel as if I'm standing on this great . . . you know the opening shot of *The Sound of Music*? Well I'm standing on that green, Swiss hill and I'm looking down into a most enormous forest. Now when I say I don't ever refer to anything (if it's a classic) that anyone else has ever done with it, it's because I think that if I do that (I suppose it's rather arrogant of me) it'll get in the way of an instinctive reaction, and I'm only a creature of impulse and instinct. Only. I'm no creature of intellect whatsoever.

So during this period, which might be weeks or months or whatever, this person inside obviously never stops working.

When rehearsals start, when I first talk about the play, it's only then that I enter the forest. I go down the hill and I'm in the forest; and although I know it's all trees I can't tell which tree is which.

103

PB	Do you not do any deliberate homework at all before rehearsals start?
JD	No. None at all.
PB	So your pre-rehearsal work is subliminal?
JD	Yes. I didn't know for a long time that it happened like that but I realise now that it does: that there is a kind of subliminal thing inside me that must start thinking about it. And being in *The Importance of Being Earnest* proved that conclusively. What happened there was I said I couldn't be in it because of a holiday we'd planned, so Peter Hall said, "Well, you can have your holiday because you're not in Act Two." So after three weeks of rehearsal Michael and I packed our tent and went off to the West of Scotland where I had two divine weeks of never sleeping for one single night, because by then (a) I didn't know the lines, (b) I didn't know how to play it and (c) they were all rehearsing back in London. I couldn't bear it. But . . . When I came back we did a run-through that afternoon and Peter said to me afterwards, "Perhaps I should tell everyone to go off for two weeks into their tents." And I swear to you, I'd taken the script, but I'd never even opened the cover. I'd never touched it. But I wouldn't have gone without it. And the night we came back from the holiday I opened the script and went through it before I went to sleep. I think you shouldn't look elsewhere.
PB	Elsewhere than in the play itself, you mean?
JD	Yes, I think that in every play there are signposts that you find, either what you say, what somebody else says about you or the way somebody else behaves towards you.
PB	Did you, for example, get the idea of Lady Bracknell's being quite so conscious of fashion from that bit where you criticise the young girl's dress?
JD	Yes. The French maid. Lady Bracknell says, "Only an experienced French maid produces a really marvellous effect in a very brief space of time." And I think this is because she's got that person back at Upper Grosvenor Street. And also I think she wears glasses because Gwendolen says, "Mama has brought me up to be

extremely short-sighted," and I don't think Lady Bracknell would bring a very presentable girl up to wear glasses if she didn't actually have to wear them herself. John Bury's original designs for Lady Bracknell's clothes made her a very rigorous, very fat lady in glasses with a kind of up-turned po on her head. And I said to Peter, "Oh! Is that what we're going to do?" and he said, "No I don't think so." And I said, "I mean she wants a bird on the hat, doesn't she? There has to be a bird, and the hat has to be worn at a slight angle, to one side?" I was rather relieved when I saw Sir Laurence on that telly saying he had to see what the character looked like. I have to do that. Once I have seen, and know just what she looks like, then that's out of the way, it's done, and I can get on to the meat of it.

PB   When you come back after rehearsal do you do homework then?

JD   No, never. It drives Michael mad.

PB   So you work only in the rehearsal room, and a bit of this thing going on inside?

JD   A lot. A lot of that. I think there's a lot of that. But I can do anything else I like. I don't have to look at the lines.

PB   Do you like to discuss your part, and the way it is developing, with the director?

JD   No, I don't like doing that. And I never ever talk about it to Michael. I might ask him some very oblique question indeed, but he won't even know it's about the play: I have to dress it up a bit; because I have a feeling that we have a sort of valve inside us, and even if I let out just a tiny thing it's gone, it's escaped. I'd rather keep it in, like compressed air.

PB   How obedient are you to your director? Say, for example, with moves. If he gives you moves do you do them? Or do you like to be left alone?

JD   I like to be given some guidance about it: but I've got so used now to the RSC way of working where you're told where everything is and you move it yourself but have help if you need it.

PB   I thought your revelations of the nicer side of Lady Bracknell were very interesting. I've never seen that before.

JD   That's Peter Hall really. He said, "They're not just cardboard characters, penny-plain and tuppence-coloured, saying very witty things. They say them because they think they ought to say them, or they think it's outrageous to say them, or they think it's covering up some other emotion.

PB   What happens when you find yourself disagreeing with a director?

JD   Well, I'll always try to do what he says. But sometimes I find something so against my instinct that if I try to live with it it's like wearing a hair-shirt. So then I might say, "Could I show you something else? Could I just show you?" And usually, now . . . The RSC way of working, with all of us finding out a way, is ideal for me: I love it, and I love it when other actors suddenly do something. Trevor Nunn makes me feel free. He did in *The Winter's Tale* and in *Juno and the Paycock* too.

PB   Talking of *Juno and the Paycock* I remember your first entrance particularly: you came into the house and you were going to do something but you didn't do it and you went to do something else. Do you like doing things like that? Do you like things like hesitation and changing your mind and darting about: the mess of everyday life?

JD   Absolutely.

PB   The Irish accent seemed to do a lot for you.

JD   I whispered in that. I whispered for all the rehearsal period. I was so frightened with all those Irish actors around; and eventually Trevor came to me and said, "You're going to have to commit."

PB   Do you find one thing, like an accent, or the kind of things which Geoffrey Hutchings sometimes does with a physical mannerism, or Anna Massey's leaning forward a bit in *The Importance*; do you find one thing can open doors for you?

JD   The best one thing I ever had was during the holiday in

Scotland. We visited Inveraray. And I looked at the castle. It was a windy, wet day and I remembered the whole incident of the Duchess of Argyll and the Duke of Argyll; but it wasn't till the final week of the holiday, the last few days, that I thought, I know just who I'm going to base Lady Bracknell on: Margaret, Duchess of Argyll. She is a great society beauty and had been a very lovely debutante; and there was the scandal, you know . . . And I thought, that's who I'm going to base her on.

PB How set are your performances? Do you like changing things?

JD Yes. And I think, ooh, gracious, gracious; and that happens a lot in *Other Places*. It's totally free, like no play I've ever done. It's because of Pinter's writing. Once I start that fifty minutes I'm like a mouse on a wheel: I'm on a track that I can't get off; it won't let go of me, it's like something pulling me into a cage. I've never felt it so strongly in a play before. I mean you know how rigorous *The Importance* is: symmetrical, beautifully orchestrated, and within that orchestration there are a few places you can go, but not many. But in the Pinter, the places you can go are legion. So if I have notes after one performance, they simply wouldn't apply to the next. So I've never had notes, ever. It's always changing.

PB Do you let it change in performance or do you sometimes think in advance what you might like to change?

JD Never. Never in advance.

PB Do you get less satisfaction from the comparative exactness of Lady Bracknell?

JD No. No I don't. In a way I don't get any satisfaction from the Pinter play. I just feel very tired at the end of it. It's very rare now, much rarer than it was when I was younger and didn't know the pitfalls so much, that I come off the stage and feel: well that's the best I can do up to this present moment. Until tomorrow. But I haven't had that feeling for years. I had it last for one night, one night only, in *Juno and the Paycock*. And I came out and I thought: that is all I can do with that – for the time being.

107

PB   Do you ever give a mechanical performance?

JD   No. No. I don't. I don't think anybody can, really.

PB   People do, though, don't they?

JD   Well I think pride takes over in a way. I think: oh, my God, I mustn't let the side down.

PB   How important to you is being in voice, and do you do any work on it before you go to the theatre?

JD   No. If you've got a voice like mine you're never in voice. When I have a cold people don't notice. I never knew I had this voice until I first heard it and I said, "That's not me." No. The only voice exercises I do are in my bath beforehand – I have the luxury of a bath at the National – and I lie in the bath every night, and I do a lot of Clifford Turner, you know – niminy piminy – before Lady Bracknell. At the final dress rehearsal, we were allowed to ask a few friends to it, and after the line "He seems to have great confidence in the opinion of his physicians", I said, "Hoorallypallyleeleeleeleepooblyooblyoobly", or some such rubbish. And it got a belter of a laugh. And we shrieked.

PB   How important do you think the off-stage life of an actress is? I don't mean keeping up appearances, looking after yourself in that way, but looking after yourself as a person, because everything that you are shows?

JD   Michael says that you can't ever be more on a stage than you are as a person in life. I used to disagree with him. But now I think he's quite right.

PB   Do you like to get to know the company you are acting with well, off stage as well as on?

JD   Oh yes. I like to check up on people. I don't like just meeting them on the stage. I like to know about them. I like to know their business. It's kind of essential. I'm always very unconfident and shy of meeting actors I don't know. I can bluff it out. But I actually don't like it. Therefore, as at Stratford, when a new company comes together, you've got twelve weeks to do two plays. But that twelve weeks I believe contains six weeks of just getting to know and relax with everybody so that

108

eventually you are able to remove every bit of clothing, and laugh at yourself and everybody else. If you're going to be inhibited in front of everybody and not dare to make a fool of yourself then you will never get to anything. Unless you can push the boat out too far, there's no point in calling it back.

Alec McCowen

I interviewed Alec McCowen on Friday 28 January at his flat in Kensington. He was not in a run of a play at the time, but was giving intermittent performances of *The Gospel According to St Mark* at the Queen Elizabeth Hall; and he always seems to have a lot of ideas coming up to the boil.

*

AMcC   I guess I'm much more prepared now when I go to a first rehearsal than I used to be. It depends on the director, though: if it's a director I trust then maybe I won't do anything like as much work, but if it's a director I don't know, or I'm not sure I can totally trust, I will do a good deal of preparation; also, as I get older, there's simply the memory factor, and I do like to become fairly acquainted with the words before rehearsals start. For instance, for the play about Hitler, *The Portage to San Cristobal of AH*, which I did a year ago, I had learnt the whole of a twenty-five minute speech in advance because I thought it would take the entire period of rehearsal to, as you might say, put the expressions in.

PB   You had a different voice for that performance. It can be dangerous when actors change their voices, because so often it doesn't come off. With you it did. Where did that low, gutteral voice come from?

AMcC   I didn't set out to change my voice; it just happened. It startled me, and people used to say "Doesn't it hurt your throat?" It didn't, I suppose, because it happened naturally. I think it became confirmed when I saw a film clip of Hitler not long before we opened and I noticed, above all else, that his voice came not from his chest, nor from his stomach, but from his bowels. But I didn't do an impersonation, and couldn't "put it on" now. Most of the work I do now (I didn't use to do this) is concerned almost entirely with understanding: understanding what the play is, and what the part is in my own terms. I have to understand the situations and the other characters totally within my own experience. Because I cannot *imagine* what it is like being a king or a pope or Hitler or whatever it is I'm playing, I have to relate it to things within myself. When I was a young actor I disguised myself: I dressed up and hid myself under make-up and costumes and funny walks and funny voices and everything, and this went on for years and years. But then there came a point . . . well, it's a journey isn't it? A long, long journey. I met Vivian Matalon and he influenced me greatly. And now, as I say, I just work for understanding, and search for total clarity. I find this releases me physically: I mean if there's any nervousness, if there's any confusion, if there's any unsureness about what I'm doing, there's going to be tension and then my body won't do what it's told.

PB   So you like to go to the first rehearsal prepared with this rather penetrating understanding of the play and your part in it?

AMcC   Yes; yet I find the first rehearsal the most terrifying part of the job. I always dread it.

PB   On account of meeting the people?

AMcC   No, on account of exposing myself for the first time. I don't know what it is that makes me so extraordinarily self-conscious after so many years, but I am; I'm like a teenager among adults: I think I'm going to be found out in some way when I open my mouth. Yes. The

111

beginning is the most terrifying of all. And the next terrifying thing is letting go. Especially if it is a part which requires extremes of behaviour. I find all that much more terrifying now than First Nights.

PB   What do you expect from a director?

AMcC   I like him to have done a certain amount of work before rehearsals start, certainly in the physical sense, so he has some idea of how a play should look. Then there's something to work on. Otherwise the rehearsals become anarchic, and I hate that because one starts being directed by the actors with the loudest voices: "Why doesn't he do this?" and, "If I go there, then he can be there," and that sort of thing. I can't rehearse under those conditions. It's agony if actors start directing each other.

PB   Are you ever tempted to do it yourself?

AMcC   Oh yes. I'm tempted. Often. But I try to resist it. Perhaps I try in devious ways, like slipping in an idea quietly in the coffee break. I like a director who gives a good deal of help at the beginning but who also gives a good deal of freedom for one, two or three weeks, by which time I will have explored all sorts of avenues, all sorts of ways of doing it; and by, say, the fourth week of rehearsal I'll have no perspective. That is when I need a director to say, "No, not that one, that one. The way you were doing it the second week was the best." I need a selecting man, a selecting genius, I suppose.

PB   Have you ever found one?

AMcC   Well, in recent work I found Michael Rudman superb with *The Browning Version* at the National. His best notes were his last ones; maybe for other actors it would have thrown them, that he would suddenly come up at the last minute and say, "You do not need that pause, you don't need to strive so hard for that effect, you don't need to make that point so clearly, trust this, trust the other." He was marvellously selective. And very sensitive.

PB   Do you ever get stuck with a part?

AMcC   Oh yes, often.

PB   What do you do?

AMcC   Well ... I've had great help in the past from what
         Vivian Matalon used to call "as ifs". They can be so
         remote from the play itself that anybody knowing
         what was going on in my head would be extremely
         startled. I found the Fool in *King Lear* a most difficult
         part because the lines are practically incom-
         prehensible nowadays and because we're not quite
         sure what a Fool is. He's not Morecambe and Wise.
         There's no counterpart today. I couldn't get near the
         part. It was gobbledygook. Or it was until I found an
         "as if", which was simply recalling myself as a small
         boy, when my father, who was the "as if" for King
         Lear, would come home from work tired, angry,
         spikey, often very bad-tempered, and I used to keep
         him sweet; I used to amuse him, and tried to stop the
         row with my mother about the food being late or not
         what he wanted or whatever. I would cavort about
         and make him laugh. It's strange how vivid childhood
         memories are: I work from them a great deal. And
         once I'd remembered that, the part lost all its stress for
         me. The struggle went out of it.

         And I found Malvolio, when I did it in the BBC
         Television Shakespeare series, difficult because I had
         too much of a mental picture of this stately, pompous,
         slow-moving person ...

PB   Because of performances of it you'd seen?

AMcC   Well it started at school. We were taught that
         Malvolio is like this, Hamlet is like that. It was a sort
         of brain-washing. And so, when we were rehearsing, I
         knew my Malvolio was a cliché-character and I
         couldn't find any life in it. Until I realised two things.
         First of all that he's a servant and he must be a good
         servant: he's got a very good job. That wasn't much
         help though. The second thing was an "as if". And I
         remembered it when I was thinking about his re-
         lationship with Olivia. I remembered working with

Vivien Leigh in *Antony and Cleopatra* in New York. She was the most beautiful, glamorous woman I've ever met or worked for; and there were a few of us young actors in the company and we all were behaving in a most ridiculous fashion trying to please Vivien Leigh, trying to get her to smile at us, trying to get a few words from her. So before going on in *Twelfth Night* I would do this substitution: that I was going on to get the approval, to get the love, of Vivien Leigh. And immediately the whole rhythm changed: from being a slow, stately, pompous man, I became fussy, and would rush to get the chair in place for her, rush to get the cushion and plump it up, and push back other people and not let them get near her. So thinking of Vivien Leigh brought the part to life. I had been a messenger in *Antony and Cleopatra* and I had one marvellous scene directly with Vivien Leigh, in which I had to tell her that Antony had married. And she had to slap my face. She was a very technical actress and she required me to be in exactly the same place and to say the lines in exactly the same manner at every performance, and once or twice I was hauled over the coals for being an inch out of position. And the night I ducked when she hit me . . . well, I'd seen this bracelet she was wearing had slipped down to her wrist and I knew I was going to get really smashed in the chops, so I ducked; and of course I got hell from Vivien Leigh. Quite rightly I suppose. But I was so stupidly besotted with her that although I was working with her I would wait at the Stage Door to see her leave the building. So she was an enormous help to me in *Twelfth Night* years later.

PB   Any more "as ifs" you've used?

AMcC Well yes. This is a geographical one. I don't think I was particularly good as Hamlet . . . I couldn't get a line on it which suited me, and I was too old for it . . .

PB   In Birmingham, was this?

AMcC Yes and that was the great point about it. I was basing

114

my performance chiefly on the line "Denmark is a prison", because I think Hamlet had escaped from that prison, he'd got to university at Wittenberg, and I think the enforced return to Denmark was immensely galling to him. I think he had a contempt for Denmark, for the Court, for nearly everybody in the play. They were small-town people, they were suburban, and he was trapped in this prison. Well I did *Hamlet* after playing on Broadway for nine months in *Hadrian VII*; and to return to Birmingham, the old, dirty Birmingham rep., in the drizzle, and to leave the theatre totally unrecognised after all the fuss of New York, all the glamour: this helped me very much as an "as if" in playing Hamlet. Denmark was Birmingham.

PB   When you're in a long run, do you change much?

AMcC Well, I have about five different versions which I will call upon to stop me from getting stale. They still don't, but nevertheless ... I will have an evening when I think solely about my relationship with the other actors, to remind me not to go over the top and that I'm actually talking to the people on the stage with me. Or I will ask myself, "What is the verb for what I am doing? Am I flirting with somebody, am I intimidating somebody?" and so on. Or I think of the intentions: I think of what I want to achieve. My favourite version, though, which I can't use too often, is what I call the "fourth-wall" version, when I spend the entire performance shutting out the audience, and giving myself total freedom, as if I'm in a room, alone, where there's no temptation to be good. No temptation to be impressive. It's marvellously releasing.

PB   It sounds as if getting stale is a hurdle for you. Is it hard, keeping fresh?

AMcC Harder and harder now, yes, because as I get older, the thought of doing things over and over again makes me angry. I mean, it's a way of earning a living, but I feel I'm putting my head in the sand. I resent it, and I

115

think the resentment creeps into my work now, to its detriment.

PB   What's your worst failing?

AMcC Just being phoney. Phoneyness. I love acting badly. Who is to say what is good or what is bad, but I would love to be a completely technical, calculating actor who was just enjoying himself. It's painful that to act well is just sheer hard work, and not very enjoyable. Except at the moment of discovery.

Edward Petherbridge

Edward Petherbridge came to my home to talk on Monday 31 January. He had just finished playing Feste in *Twelfth Night* for a tour of the Far East culminating in a short season at The Warehouse, Earlham Street. Emily Richard, his wife, had played Viola in the same production; and in the famed production of *Nicholas Nickleby*, she had been Nicholas's sister Kate, while Edward was Newman Noggs.

*

EP   It's such a social thing, being an actor. It's so easy to get impatient, but you have to try, and not let the grit of people's differences or their selfishnesses or their hang-ups get in the way, while you're busy dealing with a hang-up of your own, perhaps, and building up your working relationship with the director. And it's not unknown for *that* to be a minefield.

PB   Do you do much work before rehearsals start? Do you like to go well prepared?

EP   I do. I do like to. But I often don't. I sit and think. In the bus or in the car. I think it's very bad to turn up without having read anything about the period if it's a period play, or the background if it's specialised in any way. Sometimes observation of real people in particular jobs or situations is necessary beforehand. I like to have some coherent vision to contribute even if it's going to be modified in rehearsal.

PB   So you like to do as much research as you can?

EP   Oh yes. Of course with a few directors, Trevor Nunn for instance, research is contained within the rehearsal period as well. For example, for *Three Sisters* we did individual projects. He gave each of us a subject, like life in Moscow, or life in Perm, which was the town we chose, because it was a long way from Moscow: I mean it's important to know how far away it is and how hard it is to get to Moscow from there. It's about five hundred miles, I think. Or more; I forget now. Other subjects were travel, education, the army, religion, living conditions, local industries. When we had all read up our particular subject, we came back and shared it. And of course it's a very good way not only of building up a background to the play, but of getting to know everybody you'll be acting with.

PB   If there is a book about it, for example there was a book about Newman Noggs, would you read it?

EP   That example is a bit difficult, because, yes, there was a book about Newman Noggs, I think: unfortunately he called it *Nicholas Nickleby*. It was immensely useful. It must have been torture for David Edgar, who did the adaptation, because everybody kept saying, "Well, of course, in the book . . ." There it all was, chapter and verse.

PB   Did you make any specific requests for things which David Edgar hadn't included?

EP   Well, one I can remember. When Nicholas gets back from Yorkshire, penniless, having beaten Squeers and befriended Smike, Noggs starts to give him advice about caution and moderation – then suddenly bangs the table and says, "Damn it, I'm proud of you! I'd have done the same thing myself!" Very illuminating about Noggs, although the scene wasn't long enough to merit setting a table so I banged a chair.

PB   Did you do projects, as you had done for *Three Sisters*?

EP   Oh yes. We had a very long run-up to the rehearsal period, because we didn't have a play to start with. About six weeks, we had.

PB What was your project?

EP For *Nicholas Nickleby* we did it in pairs, so there were twenty projects. I did mine with Emily. We researched the theatre of 1838, because of the Crummles company. We took lots and lots of photographs of old prints of actors and theatres and plans and things, and then made them into slides, and found some music which was right, and some facts and figures, and gave a twenty-five minute magic-lantern show.

PB But neither of you played one of the actors.

EP No. The parts hadn't been assigned yet. I thought I might be one of them, but I wasn't.

PB How did your characterisation of Newman Noggs arrive?

EP There were many sources. The famous drawings of Phiz gave me an image. They were caricatures of course, but I thought if I can capture some of the reality inside the caricature, it would be a good thing to do and luckily I was the right kind of shape to do it: I mean long and thin. And then there was all his history, suggested here and there in the book and barely hinted at in the play. David Edgar's dramatic telegrams were a marvellous exercise in economy. And then . . . I suppose the imaginative part was imagining him in his attic on his own, before he'd met Nicholas, or even after he'd met him. Newman Noggs spent hours in his little room, having his drink, fanning the four or five coals in his grate and feeling cold, and thinking about his past or trying to forget it. And I had to ask myself: how does he get from one minute to the next? How does he put up with it? Does he switch off, and does he think about other things? How did he cope with being so solitary, not only when he was alone, but at work too. Thinking about all that helped with his physical attitude: how he stood, how he was, how he stood inside his body.

PB Did you have a red nose? Was that because of drink?

EP Yes . . . no, it was because of a little bit of lake I put there . . . yes, he was described as having a red nose. I worried about that red nose because of the clown suggestion in it; all these things can become clichés. Then I had to think: find what the cliché is, then try to discover the truth that underlies the cliché, and then do it so that the audience can't even see the cliché. I call this process "making it organic", so they can't see the joins and I can't feel them either.

PB How much are you influenced by your interest in mime?

EP A lot. Though I have a kind of dread about this because a caustic American actor said to me, when he'd seen *Nickleby* in New York, "I take it that you've studied mime, judging from your performance." I didn't like that. It ought not have shown up as a style, though I am certainly interested in acting styles which use obvious artifice.

I've just been to China and watched nine- to sixteen-year-old children being taught how to act. At the Peking Opera everything is traditional and is still being handed on intact despite the Cultural Revolution: the way they hold their hands, tilt their heads, the way they take a step, hold their feet. Every single thing is taught; and the exercises they are given are to do with fighting, singing, speaking and dancing. They achieve a completely received technique which takes care of . . . their eyebrows, everything. And yet they imbued what they were doing with a great deal of personal involvement. When we came into the room, with interpreters and all, they were in the middle of a scene and they didn't falter because of us: their concentration was so complete. I do like the kind of theatre which depends on great artifice, on stylisation, on the extremes that the performer can be called upon to come up with.

PB What is the furthest extreme you have gone to in your acting?

EP I was once in a production by Tyrone Guthrie of *Volpone*. And many of the characters in that play are named after animals: Volpone, the fox, and Voltore, the vulture, which was me. I was sent off to the zoo in Regents Park to

120

look at vultures. And I thought, my God, this is just up my street on account of my interest in movement; and ages before I'd played animals and things at theatre school a little bit, and here I was, going to look at a real vulture, and to try to speak Ben Jonson as a vulture. It proved to be very difficult. I mean, Guthrie was in love with what I was doing physically and he used to say things like, "Fly up on to the bed," you know, with Volpone lying in it, "go on, fly on to it!" But he didn't like the voice. "You're not sepulchral enough for a vulture," he said. And of course Ben Jonson is very difficult: you can understand it, just, when you read it, but you can't understand it when you're actually saying it. At least that's what I found, especially when I was trying to combine a human being with a vulture so that the join wouldn't show.

One of the things I liked about working with Guthrie was that he had a real sense of fun and he would prod us all to go over the top which is one of the things I usually don't like doing. I like restraint. It's been the undoing of me a lot of the time.

PB   Why has it been the undoing of you?

EP   Laurence Olivier said to me, just as I was about to leave the National Theatre, "You're very subtle and unusual, but I'd like to see you come out more. Raise the flag more."

PB   Do you think you ought to come out more?

EP   I've always thought it important that if you can you should suggest rather than emphasise, so that you don't tell the audience what you're doing, you let them have fun discovering it. I've thought that ever since I was at drama school. I don't know where I got it from. Perhaps, in the past, that has made me afraid of the bold statement sometimes, and bold statements are necessary because without them subtlety has nothing to show up against.

PB   Do you ever feel inadequate? What do you do when things go wrong? Do you have remedies?

EP   I think remedies are very important. I had a difficult time when I was rehearsing Vershinin in *Three Sisters*: a crisis of confidence. I felt eighteen most of the time. Absurd. As well as having a thing about looking younger than I was because of what people had said, I had a thing about being thin. And Vershinin's a colonel, for God's sake, in the Russian army.

PB   And the remedies?

EP   The remedy was to say to myself: Look. You've only got this equipment. That's what you've got to do it with. They did ask you. They haven't suggested recasting. So. Now then. You must not concentrate on these difficulties. You must not let the rehearsal period and then the performances be marred by allowing these worries to take root and become destructive. You must take a Zen attitude, to live in the moment. *You* (because they've chosen you), *you* come in, you say these things and you look at that woman and you say, my goodness you remind me of so-and-so, and you say, what a wonderful room. You go from one thing to another. One by one. Just the things you have to do. Don't worry about how you're looking or how you stand (though of course these things are important). Just concentrate on feeling happy. As if you're invited the audience to a party. Even if you're a bit wrong, only if you are happy and confident can you be acceptable or useful to an audience.

PB   You act quickly. Do you do that deliberately?

EP   Yes. I think I've always acted fast. I remember Olivier, again, saying, not to me but to someone else, "You mustn't waste the audience's time."

PB   You said that things like how you stand and how you look are important. Do you still do much work off-stage to get these, and perhaps more inner things, right?

EP   I have bouts of doing things: I'll jog for a bit, or swim for a bit; I've even lifted weights for a bit. I'll do some old movement exercises or voice exercises for a bit. Topping up, really. It's awful, isn't it, because it sounds as if one is a prize garden, which one is continually weeding and hoeing and putting compost on.

PB   But actors and actresses are stared at, aren't they? And isn't all this part of feeling happy on the stage?

EP   Yes. One is one's own instrument; and intellectually and emotionally and in every way one has to be a good vessel for all the things one has to do.

PB   Are there untrodden paths you'd like to tread?

EP   I think one goes to rehearsals with the backlog of all the things one has ever done before. I mean I know why they've cast me and I know what they expect. And nine times out of ten I'll give them what they expect. I'd love to surprise them.

PB   How?

EP   Well. I suppose I've played what is laughingly known as a large range of parts. And I suppose really I'd like to get away from all these eccentrics: clapped-out, benign creatures, clowns, intellectuals, poetic lovers, scholars. Recently I played an ordinary chap in a television play. An ordinary chap in the present. I liked that. And I'd like to do more plays which are about now, and about the problems which are to do with living in *this* world, and where I could come on dressed as I am now, maybe, and be natural. Though to be natural is just another kind of artifice.

Anna Massey

Anna Massey came to talk to me at home on 9 February. Like Judi Dench she was at that time appearing in *The Importance of Being Earnest* and *Other Places* at the National Theatre.

*

AM   Vivian Matalon was a great influence on me. His theories changed my attitude to work and to rehearsing. He kept saying, "Don't be general: be specific."

PB   What do you think he meant by that?

AM   Well, after meeting him I was lucky enough to be directed by Max Stafford-Clark in the Irish version of *The Seagull* at the Royal Court Theatre and Max put into practice what Vivian had said. He told us to "play the action" of a line and not to "demonstrate" it. You can have a simple line like, "I love you." Then you have to decide, within the context of the play, what you want to *do*, what the *action* is behind the line: in this case it could be to seduce, to provoke; there are lots of verbs to choose from. And in the early rehearsals for *The Seagull* Max used to take passages of the play, and ask us to say what the verb was before each line. We all did it. I mean, say my character was Anna and you're Peter: I get up and say "Anna provokes Peter," and then say the line.

PB   You obviously react strongly to directors. Was Max Stafford-Clark an ideal one for you?

AM   A milestone. He took away a lot of the wasteful fret I often

124

get into in rehearsals. After a while we stopped saying the actions and just did them and let in a lot of other things, but at least we knew what we were doing. We could all see the scenes from everybody's point of view, so it led to good teamwork and stopped anybody from giving a solo performance. It also made us economical, and I like economy. It helped us, when we came to perform the play, to keep it fresh. I swear it was as fresh at the end of the run as it had been at the beginning.

PB   Do you say "I" or "she" when you talk about your part?

AM   Vivian Matalon says you must say "I". I'm sure you should. The part has to become *you*. What was it John Gielgud said? – "Ninety per cent of you is there anyway."

PB   Do you like to do your own placing?

AM   It depends on the director. Max Stafford-Clark sort of says he doesn't know how to do it, but of course he does. If everything's going right he shouldn't have to say, "Sit on that sofa," or "Get up on that line." It should just happen; and Max made us so aware of our relationships with each other – including the man who brought on my suitcase: I knew exactly what I thought of him and he of me – that all the moves came out of the actors. I like that, especially since I think actors are unselfish. On the whole.

PB   How do you start to work on a part?

AM   Well, first of all I read the play to decide whether I want to play the part or not. This is the most important read because my instinct's at work. Actually I didn't do that for Miss Prism, because everybody said when I was offered it, oh what a good part for you, oh you'll be very good. So I said yes. Then I read it and thought, I can't do it. It's not me at all. What have I let myself in for? I mean, Miss Prism is eccentric and I'm not. Well, not in the same way. I mean, I'm not a born eccentric like Margaret Rutherford was. Margaret Rutherford didn't have to act eccentricity: it was something she brought on with her. So the first thing I had to do was pretend the play had never been done before and Margaret Rutherford had

125

never been Miss Prism. Actually of course the word "eccentric" is a generality and not much help. It's like saying a character is mad, or ill or whatever. You have to work out what these generalities mean. So I worked out a biography. I do that with every part.

PB   Before rehearsals start?

AM   Oh yes. Always. I like to know what my parents were like, and whether I have brothers or sisters. And I cast them. From old friends, new friends, people I've seen in the street. Then I can see them. In my mind's eye. Images. I like to know the house where I was born, the school I went to and, most definitely, where the play takes place.

PB   So what was Miss Prism's biography?

AM   I worked out a story which made me fifty-two. I'm too young for the part, you see. And I worked out the youngest I could be was fifty-two. In the play there's a line, "An injury received from the upsetting of a Gower Street omnibus," so I worked out that I went to college in Gower Street and fell in love with a German student: I was writing my novel at the time, and became a governess when I was twenty-two. I was born in Leamington and I made Patrick Moore my father. My mother had died because I couldn't think of a mother. And because we all talk so much about Germany in the play I thought that I had spent quite a lot of time in Heidelberg, because I'd been there once; so I cast myself as a governess there.

PB   Teaching foreign students? Is that what made you speak so precisely?

AM   I don't know. You see when I work out these biographies I don't know what the result will be. I don't play the result. For example, my son came to the play and said, "I love the voice." And I said, "What do you mean, the voice?" And he said, "It's so high." But I didn't, honestly, know that it had happened.

PB   Where did the slight stoop come from?

AM   The corsets I had to wear.

PB   And the dainty step?

126

AM   From a walk in Holland Park with a friend when we talked a lot about the play.

PB   I've been listening to you today, and on the telephone, and I've noticed that you speak more quickly and flowingly in everyday life than you tend to in plays. Do you do that because you think actors and actresses have a duty to protect the language, and speak very clearly?

AM   Daniel used to say I over-enunciate. Of course I'm often cast in parts which demand quite precise English. Harold Pinter, for example, writes very precisely. In *Family Voices* I have to say: "I hear your father's step on the stair. I hear his cough. But his step and his cough fade. He does not open the door." It's not naturalistic dialogue. But maybe we do it with too much reverence.

PB   Do you agree with Daniel?

AM   I suppose I do. There are only a few more performances to go of *A Kind of Alaska*: perhaps I shall work on it in that. Could stop the reverence coming out. It might have something to do with a fear of fluffing. I used to have that a lot. It's less now, thank heavens.

PB   Yes I have that too. Especially on those nights when you have to be careful, like First Nights, or friends in front. Do you like to know when friends are out front?

AM   Oh no. I absolutely hate it.

PB   Why?

AM   It distracts me from the world of the play. It can be a block, preventing me from entering that world.

PB   We start, in our childhood, by showing off, don't we? That's why we become actors. But then it changes and we can become shy and self-conscious. Did you start by showing off?

AM   Oh yes. And the first play I did, *The Reluctant Debutante*, I just thought, on the opening night on tour, oh this is heaven; and then the Tuesday night the same; and then on the Wednesday afternoon I dried, and I thought, oh I don't like doing this, I don't think I'll bother to come to London. And then I started getting nervous and realised that doors don't always open, and things go wrong.

127

PB   What do you do when things go wrong?

AM   Well, I write myself a lot of notes after performances. I set myself goals.

PB   Such as?

AM   Hands stiller. At the drop of a hat I can be conducting an orchestra.

PB   And?

AM   Lightness. It's so easy to force things in a long run. In *The Importance* I lost a very big laugh, and I said to Paul Rogers, "Why have I lost that laugh?" and he said, "I don't know, you seem to be doing it in exactly the same way." So I gave myself notes: lighter, spontaneity – I often write that word down – often to no avail – and I suddenly remembered what I'd done at the first preview. The line was "I think, dear Docter, I will have a stroll with you. I find I have a headache after all." This after I've just denied having a headache. And I remembered I used to do it with such joy, almost a little skip, and that's funny.

PB   And how had you been doing it when you lost your laugh?

AM   Very sadly. As though I had a headache.

PB   And where did that hilarious walk towards Lady Bracknell in the last act come from? It's so bold. When you approach her with your head turned right round the other way?

AM   That came during the previews. One night I just felt it's as though I'm being drawn to somebody and I don't want to look at her.

PB   What had you done before?

AM   Just walked with my head down.

PB   And did you get a laugh the first time you tried the new way?

AM   No.

PB   But it was a hoot the night I saw it.

AM   Oh, sometimes it gets a round. It varies colossally.

PB   When you're on television, do you like to watch yourself?

AM   No, I hate it.

PB   Why?

128

AM   I think I'll catch myself not listening properly or something, or that I'll be acting too much, or being jerky. It's the same really, I suppose, as my dread of people being out front. I've got this dread of criticism. Especially from people I admire. They have to have my respect and admiration and then I dread their being out front. Part of me shies away from the notes they may give me, but part of me is grateful because I can learn from them. And there's something in there that I haven't quite sorted out.

PB   Do you enjoy acting more now than you used to?

AM   I've always had a love-hate relationship with it; in the seventies, about the time of Simon Gray's *Spoiled*, which I was in at the Haymarket, and David Hare's *Slag*, I felt seriously like giving the whole thing up. I had such a fear about acting in the theatre that I thought, well, I can't do it, there's no enjoyment left, I can't bear it, I'll just do television. But the fear came with me to television. So I went to an analyst.

PB   Was it self-consciousness that made you dislike it so much?

AM   No. It was panic.

PB   About what?

AM   Well, panic seizes everything up. It's like frozen, blocked drains. Nothing happens. Everything freezes. I suppose it was self-consciousness. Yes. I didn't know it at the time.

PB   How did this affect your acting?

AM   I was at my unhappiest when I took over from Penelope Keith in *Donkeys' Years*. I mean, the fact of taking over didn't help; but no director in the world at that time, 1977, would have got through to me. I was very resistant.

PB   To directors?

AM   To everything: to life. What your life is like affects your acting. I think your approach to life is what is going to come out as your approach to art. I'm happier in life now so I'm a happier actress.

PB   Do you work on life?

AM   Yes. And on acting, all the time. I think it's very very

129

hard. And I'm not at all like Judi Dench who sometimes says, "Oh, I can't wait to get on there." I've never said that in my life.

Wyn Jones

When I interviewed Wyn Jones at home on Wednesday 23 February I asked him to concentrate on his most recent work: a six-month tour of Alan Ayckbourn's *Sisterly Feelings* preceded by a season of fortnightly rep. at the Leas Pavilion Theatre, Folkestone.

*

WJ In a fortnightly rep. a good average working day, well, it'll depend a bit on how late you stayed up the night before – going out for a drink after the show, or learning, or most probably both – but a good average day will start with a couple of hours before rehearsal at ten o'clock to go through the lines you've only just learnt. You don't wake up with them, you see: you've only had one sleep-time on them, so you have to refresh yourself and go through them. It becomes part of going to the theatre warmed up and feeling on top of things. I like to do voice exercises, too, and things like that, though in digs it's a bit difficult to do too much of a vocal warm-up on account of the other people there. And some physical exercises, too: relaxing, stretching and perhaps going for a quick walk.

But as the season goes on and you get tireder, it's harder to do all this. You crawl out of bed and just try to get to rehearsal on time.

PB For the first rehearsal of each play, did you have a read-through?

WJ   Oh no. There was no time for that.

PB   Do you think it's right, in a rep., for the director to tell you what the moves are going to be?

WJ   Absolutely. I think it would be chaos if he didn't. You'd spend the whole of the first week working out where you were going. I mean, you might get better results for yourself, but you'd waste so much rehearsal time for everybody else. It's especially necessary for the director to be strict if there are eight people on the stage; if it's a duologue you can be more approximate to start with because there can be more give and take.

PB   How long did it take to do the placing?

WJ   We'd block the whole play the first morning. The Wednesday. Then of course we'd have a matinee and an evening performance of the current play.

PB   And then how did rehearsals go?

WJ   Well, the next day, the Thursday, we'd know the first section and break it down, then Friday the next section and Saturday the next. So the first week was spent learning the play as best we could. During the second week, if we rehearsed mornings only, we could use the free afternoons, apart from matinee days of course, for going over what we'd rehearsed in the morning but also for reading the play for the following fortnight.

PB   Did you always have afternoons off? I did when I was in rep. If you don't, it's a twelve-hour working day, isn't it?

WJ   No we didn't always have afternoons off. Usually, but not always. Because there's so little rehearsal time many people, including of course the director, are tempted to go on into the afternoon. This happens especially when everybody's enthusiastic about a play, as we all were about Mike Leigh's *Abigail's Party*. We used to go on with that till five or five-thirty. It was far too much. It's a very intense play, all about people driven to their limits; I was Laurence, and, you know, having a heart attack five times in an afternoon, well, it's very tiring. Then I'd go to the digs for tea and a very short nap and go back to do another large part, in *Butterflies Are Free* it was, in the

132

evening. If you over-rehearse you pay for it at the end of the season; and I think you just have to pace yourself so you don't get dog-tired. All I know is that when I got to the smallest part I had during the season I was really relieved to have time off from rehearsal because I wasn't in every scene, and I thought, oh I haven't got to learn a whacking part. I mean it can become just learning after a while. Some people can gauge realistically what can happen in a fortnight. I can't.

PB Yes. The ideal is mornings only, isn't it?

WJ Yes. It gives you time to read ahead, and I think that's very important. You can think about your next character's function.

PB What do you mean by "function"?

WJ I like to work out how I should contrast with, or complement, the other characters. The more I understand the play, the more I can understand why my character is there. It's no good to me, although I know it is to other people, to look at the play from the standpoint of my character only, because I might misinterpret it, and interpretation is as much part of being in a play as acting in it is. This thinking about a character's function goes in somewhere. But when it comes to rehearsing I forget it, and do what I feel is right, and use my instinct: I try not to make objective decisions then, like "oh, I should be stronger, or more sinister", because I hope, by then, I've already made them.

PB There are many differences between the life of an actor in a provincial rep. and the life of a freelance in London: you don't live at home, you're working on three plays at once and you can't pick and choose your parts. Do you like the challenge of the inevitable wide range of parts, for some of which you are bound to be miscast?

WJ Absolutely. And if the general opinion seems to be that you've been all right in other plays, you can afford sometimes to be below par: of course you don't want to be bad, but you can more easily accept that you're not going to be good in everything. I try not to give in, or I give in as little as I can. I try not to say, "Oh, this part isn't me," and just rely on disguise. Edward in *The Hollow* is a diffident bear of a man, a kind, woolly teddy-bear, very gentle, a bit lumpish, a different class from me, a different age, forty or even forty-five. How was a neurotic, wiry, bouncy twenty-eight-year-old supposed to play this uncle-figure? So I decided to forget all that and think, how can *I* be gentle and diffident and avuncular at twenty-eight? I didn't want to spray my hair with grey.

PB   So you went for the qualities rather than any sort of disguise?

WJ   Yes, although I always like a little bit of disguise. And I do take great pleasure in working out what I'm going to wear. And I like to have little things that only I know about. They're like superstitions; they're like talismen. They can be little things I do off-stage, as preparation for it, or on it during the performance. For one part I liked to carry a book sticking out of my pocket; it was just a private joke really: it was a book this character would read, but it was also about the theme of the play. It was called *The Principles of Freedom in Society*, and at a matinee I was very pleased to hear someone on the front row read the title aloud. But it was also a relic of this character's untidiness; and so for the same part I had my tie not tied properly, and hair which looked as if it had been tidied by somebody else but not very well. I just like to fill my performance, and therefore myself, with physical things that I know are there like: why a wedding ring? or why a particular watch or something?

PB   Why a moustache as Laurence in *Abigail's Party*?

WJ   Oh, that was just to make myself look older. I hate stage moustaches, but in rep. there's no time to grow one. You close on a Saturday without one and open three days later with one. So I had to stick one on. And this meant, because of the spirit-gum, my upper lip had less mobility than usual. It was a terrific help, because it made Laurence's sneer into a dreadful, sidelong smile. He was so sad inside, you see, that he only smiled out of duty; and this awful triangular mouth was born at the dress rehearsal.

PB   Was Laurence one of your favourite parts there?

WJ   Yes. When I look back on the whole season I know I was better in the better plays. *Abigail's Party* is so well written it just carries you along. No lines are wasted; and when my instinct really got going I felt that the whole play was about Laurence not being loved by Beverly: life was a constant battle for him, and he says, "Not that life is easy, no, life is hard," and it *was* hard, and I connected all this to his indigestion and heart complaint, so the heart attack was inevitable.

PB   Do you find what Mike Leigh calls "running conditions", like indigestion and a heart complaint, helpful? Do you like to find encapsulations?

WJ   Yes. They're not always easy to find, though. In the poorer plays I just couldn't, and felt vague and in grave danger of losing interest. But when you're proud of a play, not necessarily the production but the play itself, like *Abigail's Party* or *Stage Struck*, and you can believe in what's being said, it's a different world altogether.

PB   But in rep., once a play's on, that's it, isn't it? You've got to start work on the next one?

WJ   Well, you do bits of work. You have to grit your teeth and get on with it.

PB   How much stage management have you done?

WJ   At various times I think I've done nearly all the jobs. I've been on the book, I've done electrics and sound and flies and props and marking the set and building the set and painting the set.

PB   Do you think it's a good thing for actors to have done stage management?

WJ   Only briefly. Only to get an understanding of what it entails.

PB   As an actor, what do you expect of the stage management?

WJ   Mostly that they don't do it grudgingly, but regard themselves as part of the team, part of the play. You want

135

them to be accurate, of course, but more than that to give you support. The person on the book is the most important of all. For example, there are ways of giving prompts: somebody can give you a prompt and at the same time manage to make you feel like an idiot for drying; somebody else might withhold a prompt for a little while because they know you really know it, and then they might give you a key word or something. And if you feel that the person on the book is interested in how the play is forming they become part of creating it.

PB   A good stage management must be very disciplined mustn't they, and be in charge?

WJ   Yes. Not let people talk in the wings or move about unnecessarily. Keep the backstage quiet.

PB   And tidy?

WJ   Yes.

PB   And visit you in the dressing-room before the show to see everything's all right?

WJ   Yes. Stick their head in. Not a long chat and expect to sit down and have a cup of tea during the half, I don't like that.

PB   Do you like to be close to the company socially?

WJ   Yes. Very. Drinks afterwards and jokes. Oh yes.

PB   What did you learn from this particular season?

WJ   Hard to say. The importance of vocal variety and things like that, basic things; the importance of everybody supporting each other and caring; but I suppose for myself I could see the harm that I did when I hated a play and went around saying so. So I tried to shut up about the things I didn't like. I mean, it could be awful: there was one play when we'd go to the pub afterwards and laugh our heads off about the rubbish we were doing and that made the next performance almost impossible to do. It was dreadful. So I thought, I won't do that again.

PB   After the season was over, you did a national tour of *Sisterly Feelings*. Here you had a part which suited you and which you had accepted in the normal way. But you had to sustain the role for six months.

136

WJ   Yes. The longest time, by far, that I've ever had to play a part.

PB   Did you feel stale as the tour continued?

WJ   No. Oddly enough. No. I realised it was possible to continue to care, to keep on trying, for a very long time. That was a surprise. But my first surprise was that acting with tried and tested people like Peter Sallis, which I had been a bit scared of, knowing that I was an unknown actor and would have to prove myself, was easier than I could possibly have imagined. I found it's easier to be good if you're with good people.

And there were nights, particularly in my scenes with Tessa Peake-Jones, when new things happened, illuminating things, and we thought, oh why have we never thought of that before? And this was particularly towards the end of the run.

And there were other nights when I would lose laughs, and wonder why. I remember vividly a night in Richmond when I got off to a poorish start, I mean it all felt like the repetition it was, and I just said to myself that old cliché, come on, be "in it" a bit more; and just saying that made some lost laughs come back.

PB   It does work, doesn't it, telling yourself stories about the characters or the play before you go on, so you can, hopefully, be "in it", as you say?

WJ   Yes, but there's a reverse side to all that. I was terribly late once getting to Birmingham on account of missing a turning, and even later one night at Cardiff when my car broke down. I got to the theatre with two minutes to spare. They were two of the best performances I ever gave. Especially the Cardiff one.

PB   Have you any theories about that? Could it be because you're on a high of excitement when you arrive, full of adrenalin, there's no worry, no preconception of possible failure that night?

WJ   Yes. The wings are dark, the stage is light, and you switch on your familiar world. After the turmoil of the journey you know where you are. Yes. It can be quite exciting

137

when it happens suddenly.

PB   What were the hardest things about touring?

WJ   Oh, the usual things when confidence goes. Bad nights. Just got to grin and bear them.

PB   What did you get most out of the experience of playing the same part for six months?

WJ   Well, it was interesting largely because it was a comedy, and people in different towns laughed in different ways and at different times.

During the rep. season I've told you about one of the directors said, "Oh you're going to hate this part because you can't be nice Wyn Jones in it. You do like to be liked, don't you?" And another time he said, "Oh, come on, you're not playing Jesus Christ in this." And this took me very much by surprise because the characters I had liked playing most were the unsympathetic ones. Of course I'd tried to identify with them and see things from their point of view. But latterly I have realised how much I do like to be liked.

PB   Was it *Sisterly Feelings* which pointed that out to you?

WJ   Yes. I always have a soft spot for whoever I am playing and I had a particularly soft spot for Stafford T. Wilkins. And the nights when the audience's laughter was affectionate laughter, when I felt they loved the character as much as I did, well, those were the best nights. I mean, there's obedient laughter and there's uninhibited, un-reserved laughter which isn't only to do with a funny line or a funny situation, it's to do with an actor or actress you like, and are willing to respond to readily. There are comedians that you like and comedians that you don't. They tell the same joke, and you laugh at the one and not at the other.

Alison Steadman

When I interviewed Alison Steadman on Friday 25 February, I asked her to concentrate, to the exclusion of everything else, on how she worked with her husband, Mike Leigh, on her part as Beverly in his play *Abigail's Party*. I had known nothing, until that winter morning at home, about Mike Leigh's method of making a play, even though he had been a student at RADA while I was still taking classes there. I didn't connect, until after the interview, his use of improvisation with mine (explained earlier in this book), possibly because he goes so much further than I had in its application. I had been amazed at his plays, *Abigail's Party* and *Goose-Pimples*: how deep they were, how extreme, how savage and how funny. But what Alison Steadman had to tell me was an eye-opener: I didn't know things like this happened.

*

AS   For *Abigail's Party* Mike chose five actors: three women and two men. He had said to me, "I'm going to do a play and I'd like you to be in it. I don't know what you'll be doing: you might do a small part, you might be the central character, I don't know. But are you willing to take that risk?" So, I said yes. Then he said to me, and to all the others, separately, "I'd like you to make a list of people that you know, either very well or just acquaintances, that aren't in the theatre, that are in this age-

139

group," – in my case it was something between, I don't know, twenty-eight and thirty-five, – "and within this certain class of society."

PB   Does he always specify that?

AS   Usually.

PB   How did he define it in this case?

AS   I can't remember exactly but probably lower middle class or working class. So I made a list and I talked about them, and when I'd described them he said, "Right. I want you to think about and work on that particular woman."

She was someone I didn't know terribly well: I knew her family and a few things about her but I didn't know much detail. Nevertheless she was the jumping-off point, the springboard. It's not to say that from then on I wanted to impersonate her: she was the start. Mike calls it, "The first mark on the canvas. You've got to start somewhere. When you paint a picture you've got to begin. And once you've made the first mark you can make the second."

Anyway. After that we all met for the first day's rehearsal. We had eight weeks, with a week of previews, and people said, "*God*, what a length of *time*!" but really, when there's not a word written yet, it's no time at all. Anyway. We all met and sat there and smiled at each other and were very apprehensive. After that we all, individually, had a session with Mike, and we each spent the next ten days or a fortnight working alone with him. First of all being that person alone. He said to me, "Where is she living?"

"At home with her parents."

"Does she have her own room?"

"Yes."

"Right. Here's her room. Let's say her parents are out, or on holiday, and she's alone. What happens? Would she read magazines?"

And so you start making decisions that give you your base.

140

"Does she work?" he said.

"Yes."

"What kind of job does she have?"

"Er . . . well . . . she's very fashion conscious, very make-up conscious, maybe she would work in a chemist's shop, selling make-up."

"Right," said Mike. "Now: it's a day when she's at home and she's alone in her room."

He sits in a corner. Very quietly. Forget about him. No pressure. Be that person. No need to do anything. Actors are so used to performing they tend to want to do a lot: make a lot of telephone calls or a cake. But that's not the job in hand, which is merely to be that person, feel like that person. What mood is she in? What day is it? It's a Saturday morning, and it's raining outside. She's on her own, she's not going out that night, she's not seeing any friends. How does she feel that day?

So that's the beginning. Then a little chat with Mike, who will stop it at some point. There's no one else in the room to watch, so you don't have to start performing and being good. I mean, sometimes it's awful: you don't feel right and you get self-conscious; but eventually a little life does begin to grow and suddenly you think, oh I am somebody different, I am beginning to think like another person and not like the actress Alison Steadman saying to herself, "I know, I'll do this bit like this because it will be right." And then there's bringing clothes into rehearsal. We had by now established that this particular woman was preoccupied by her appearance and her make-up and her hair, and so for rehearsal . . .

PB   Still alone?

AS   . . . Oh yes. In private. I was never told what was happening with the others.

PB   And always in a rehearsal room?

AS   Oh yes. Mike and I talked hardly at all about it at home. It wouldn't work.

PB   How many hours a week each?

AS   I suppose I'd have about five shortish sessions. The rest
of the time I'd do some research. For instance, we
decided that ultimately her job would be a beautician,
you know, a down-market . . . well, she'd call herself a
beautician, in fact she was selling make-up in a big store
in the West End. So I got in touch with a cosmetics
company, I think it was called Clinique, or some such
name, and asked if I could meet a personnel woman who
would tell me what training Beverly would have had and
what money she'd earn.

We had by now decided to call her Beverly, and
when I was chatting to this woman the phone went and
she answered it and said, "Oh hello, Beverly!" And
afterwards she said, "She's one of my girls, she's been out
on the circuit." They tour around the big stores. So I
spent the next few days wandering around John Lewis
and Selfridges, just watching the girls: the way they
dressed, how they behaved and spoke; and gradually
things were beginning to grow, without actually saying,
"Ah that's a good idea: I could do that." None of that.
And then, a wonderful thing happened, because there
was this girl doing a demonstration, making up a woman,
and there was a crowd round and she'd got a little
microphone tucked in the corner of her mouth, so I just
stood and watched. And I got so much: her style, her
manner, everything, the whole performance, because of
course she was giving a performance. So I went back to
rehearsal with much more information.

Then Mike set up an improvisation with Tim Stern,
who was to play Laurence. Ultimately the two characters
were married, but this impro. was about the first time
they met. Also of course it was the first time I spoke as
Beverly, and this voice came out. I still didn't know
anything about the other three people or what Mike had
been doing with them, and really I wasn't interested to
know: I was getting so involved with Beverly and her life,
and by the time I met Tim I knew so much about her that
I could answer any question about her that he might ask

me: "Are your parents alive?" and I knew. So our conversation was backed by a great deal of information, which prevents that awful thing of someone saying (as can happen in ill-prepared improvisations), "Oh isn't it cold today?" when you'd been thinking it's hot. I'm not saying all our impro.'s were good. Sometimes they were very boring. And long.

PB   How does Mike initiate an improvisation?

AS   For instance, this first one: he said to me, "Right. Get ready. Go into character. It's Monday morning, it's eight-thirty and she's going off to her new job. I want you to go outside and walk down to the tube. Then turn round, and when you come out of the tube station, come back here and this will be your new office, and when you walk into the office, if you see anyone else, they are in character." Well, for this first impro. I wasn't sure who I'd meet, but it was Tim Stern. It was Laurence. It was gradually established that Laurence invited Beverly out. Obviously a lot of the stuff we accelerated forwards, so we had chats with Mike, and he'd say, "Well, he's asked her out: where would they go?"

And Laurence would say, "For a meal."

And Mike would say, "If he suggested that to Beverly, how would she react?" I mean we talked things through, and in an hour you can have a six-week relationship: you don't have to act everything. But I knew for example that she wouldn't want to go to a Wimpy Bar, she'd want a bistro.

Then one day Mike said, "Right, they get married."

And Tim's face fell and he said, "No, I can't bear it."

But Mike said, "They get married. Now. Would it be a white wedding, would the parents be there, would it be a registry office? What would it be?"

So we talked the wedding through and we'd got them married then.

Mike said, "Where will they live? He's got a flat: would she move in?" And we decided she would, but then

143

she decided she didn't like it, so they moved to another flat; so we leapt it on, did a lot of improvisations in this new flat, like: "She's at home, she's got home from work, it's six o'clock, she's preparing the evening meal, or not, as the case may be. Go into character." We'd set up a room with pots and pans and things, even a practical television.

Then Laurence would come home and say things like, "Where's the food?"

And she'd say, "Oh sorry, I haven't had a chance to shop." And gradually it built up that they were at loggerheads most of the time because she was so pre-occupied with everything except domestic things that it drove him up the wall. She became very dissatisfied with this new flat, so eventually they bought a house in Chigwell, Essex.

PB How long had you been rehearsing by now?

AS About five weeks. And in that time we'd gone from making the list of women to being married and living in a semi in Chigwell. Mike told us about the street, how on one side the houses were 'thirties semi's and on the other they were brand new. He told us who else lived in the street, and that the people over the road were the Macdonalds; and it all became very real. We'd add new layers: did Beverly want a baby? – "No, no way" – did Laurence? – "No, never."

PB Did Laurence have his heart condition by now?

AS No.

PB Oh!

AS No. Beverly never knew about his heart condition.

PB Did he know?

AS No. As far as I was aware. He had certain symptoms, but it was always heartburn or overwork or something.

One day Mike said to me, "I want you to go into character, and I want you to go out and do some shopping." Well, we were rehearsing near Regents Park in a church hall and there were some shops not far away. He said, "I want you to go to the shops, in character, and

	then come back."
PB	In Beverly's clothes?
AS	Oh yes, with all the gear on. I mean it's the funniest thing to walk along a street as somebody else. Anyway off I went, and I saw Thelma Whiteley. Now I knew she was in the play: I didn't know what she was playing, but I knew she was another character, because she didn't look like Thelma Whiteley. So, I saw her and I sort of smiled as Beverly would, and Thelma just nodded to me and that was all that happened. And this went on for days: we kept seeing each other in the street, nodding and smiling. And something in me kept thinking, as an actress I should obviously be moving this on and talking to this other character, but I thought I can't because that's not what she would do. So I thought, no, go on trusting and keep to the truth and do what you're told, and don't think, well it would make the play better if I did this or that. Do what she would do and you can't go wrong. You can only go wrong if you start not following the rules. Anyway, eventually Beverly talked to this character, who was called Sue in the play, and said, "If you're ever passing do pop in for a coffee," because she was the sort of neighbour that Beverly would like to be friends with: a nice, middle class lady; and she also wanted to show off her home.
	And then it was established that Laurence and Beverly did their weekly shop at Sainsbury's. We actually went to Sainsbury's a few times, in character . . .
PB	Didn't you giggle?
AS	Not yet. We hadn't got to the giggling bit yet. But on one occasion Mike said, "Right. Go off in the car to Sainsbury's. Drive along so-and-so Road . . ." (in fact we went down to Finchley Road and used that Sainsbury's) ". . . park the car, go in, get all your shopping, and bring it back." The only thing was when we went shopping we couldn't buy Beverly's stuff – you know, it would be twenty quid down the drain – so Mike said we could compromise.

Anyway on the way we saw Sue standing at a bus stop. So I said, "Oh Laurence, stop, there's Sue!" It turned out her car had broken down, and she was going shopping. Mike had set the whole thing up and had said to her, "Your car's broken down, you've got to go shopping, and you've got to go on a bus." So she got in and we all went off to Sainsbury's in character. We did the shopping, and when we were standing in the check-out queue Tim saw a friend of his, an actor. And this friend said, "Tim, Tim, hello," and waved to him. Of course Tim didn't want to ignore the bloke completely, but he didn't want to break the whole thing up, so he just kind of grunted and nodded. And this bloke couldn't understand why Tim was being so rude to him. Anyway. Back we went; and this impro. went on for a long time: Sue came in for coffee, and we put the shopping away and chatted. When we'd finished Mike said, "The Ideal Home Exhibition is on at the moment. Would she like to go?" And I said, "Yes, definitely." And he said to Tim, "Would Laurence want to go?" and Tim said, "No, he wouldn't be very keen, but if she forced him he'd go." So the next day we went, in character, to the Ideal Home Exhibition and spent the whole day there.

PB Was Mike there too?

AS No. He had watched us in Sainsbury's, but he was rehearsing someone else on this day. It turned out to be one of the best days, really, because it established so much about their relationship. Beverly's life was only furniture, cosmetics, clothes and sex, so of course she was in paradise: I mean there were heart-shaped baths and things like that; and they were arguing over everything and he would say, "You have no TASTE," and "I wouldn't have that in my house." And in fact the painting that Beverly brings down at the end of *Abigail's Party*, the one with the swan with a naked man standing on it, was at the Ideal Home Exhibition, and Beverly said, "Can we buy that picture?" and we had a terrible row about it. When we got back we told Mike about it

146

and I said, "She'd go back and buy it." Mike said, "Let's leave that for now," and then he told us that the Macdonalds over the road were moving out, and a new couple had bought the house. How would Beverly react to this? So I said, "Well she'd watch all the furniture that was going in, and she'd spend a long time just watching them, weighing them up." Mike said, "They're a young couple with no family."

Next day he said, "Go into character and you're at home. It's six-thirty in the evening. Laurence is out with one of his clients." And there was a knock at the door. I didn't know who it was going to be. So I opened the door and Janine Duvitski was standing there, as Angela, and she said, "I hope I'm not disturbing you but I just wanted to say hello because we've just moved in." So I said, "Oh. No. Come in." and we did an impro.

It had been established that Beverly had watched them a lot and had taken a fancy to Tony, the husband, and had been trying to work out an opportunity for getting them over there for a nice social evening. So Beverly said to Angela, "Would you and your husband like to come over one evening for drinks?" Well we did an impro. of that and then we did another one when Sue called, and Sue told Beverly about her teenage daughter Abigail who was having a party at home that Saturday night. Now, without Mike saying anything, Beverly quickly said, "Well, why don't you pop down here and have the evening with us?" So it was agreed that we should have an evening when the three of them would arrive. The rehearsal room was set up with a record-player and drinks and food. Whatever I said Beverly would provide was brought in by the stage management.

PB   Had you chosen the furniture by now?

AS   We were still working with rehearsal furniture, but we knew what it would be. Of course, while all this was going on, Mike was working with the designer, Tanya McCallin.

PB   And you now had a full stage management?

147

AS   Yes. They were around. As we needed things like coffee and tea they brought them. Gradually we were building it up.

PB   And were the drinks real for this improvisation?

AS   Yes. For the only time. It lasted four hours. It was wonderful. The next day Mike, who was monitoring it very carefully now, said, "We've got to put a play together. After all this nonsense we've been doing for weeks, we've now got to construct a play." And he said, for the first time, "The play will take place in Laurence and Beverly's house on a Saturday evening, the night of Abigail's party." So we started with Beverly alone, and he said, "It's seven-thirty in the evening. Laurence isn't home yet. What would she have done by way of preparation for the party?" And so we started to construct the events, still using improvisation. But Mike would stop us now, and say, "Let's go back to the beginning, and when Laurence arrives don't shout at him," and he'd give us lines to speak now and build a scene as any writer would.

PB   Writing it down the while?

AS   No. Making notes, distilling what happens, paring it down. But when we started putting the play together I laughed till I cried. For a fortnight I couldn't stop. It was disgraceful: I was sure Mike would lose his temper. But I couldn't help it: it was so desperate, so awful, and so hysterically funny. Particularly when Sue came in, and we were so rude to her . . . I mean it was like throwing custard-pies at the woman. Anyway, I simmered down, and as we went on, with Mike giving us more and more lines, it was curiously easy to do, so secure we all were in our characters. But when we'd finished working through the play it lasted four hours. We'd got the basic construction, and knew when the audience had to be given this or that information; now we had to go back to the beginning and really refine, and cut out bits. And when we'd got about three-quarters of the way through Mike set up an improvisation, and he said to me, "And this is where the picture comes in." And I said, "The picture?" And he said, "Yes, the picture she saw at the Ideal Home Exhibition." And I said, "Oh yes," and he said, "She's bought it. It's upstairs in the bedroom." You see in improvisations Mike sometimes uses the technique of asking people to leave the room so they don't know some information they shouldn't know.

PB   Yes.

AS   Well. We did this impro. and Laurence said, "You bring that picture down, Bev, and I'll kill you." And I walked out and actually said the line, "Drop dead!" We were at Hampstead Theatre by this time, working in the set, and the picture was in the dressing-room. And when I came back there was Laurence on the floor. I was terribly thrown. There he was, dying on the floor and it was . . . an extraordinary moment because of this total panic.

PB   Had Mike said it to him that day?

AS   I don't know. I don't know. Obviously this condition was known to Beverly only as she would know about it in everyday life. What had been established privately between Mike and Tim I don't know, but, presumably, yes, they had talked a lot about how far his condition had gone; and it was Mike, not Tim, who said, "On this day, at this time, you have a heart attack." So we all dealt with it as our characters would. It was terribly upsetting; the rehearsal had been fun and we'd been laughing and enjoying ourselves and suddenly it was awful. It was quite a heavy morning, as I recall, and it upset Tim Stern a lot. He actually cried when the impro. had finished. He was crying for Laurence, for his character: that we do these awful things to each other. They were destroying each other, locked in this room, drinking like mad; and this is what society had produced: a man who had no choice, who was trapped by all these things. I mean, nothing was said, but we all just knew it was awful, this whole thing of these people we were playing. But the important thing is, that that was just the impro. We still had to construct the scene itself.

PB   But no script?

AS   No script. That was done well after we'd opened.

PB   So how did you set your performances, so you could repeat them?

AS   Well, by going back to the beginning, and rehearsing each section; somehow you learn it and know it.

PB   Did the performances of it vary a great deal?

AS   No. Exactly the same.

PB   Words and all?

AS   Words and all. You play it like any play. You begin to know where the laughs are, how to time them.

PB   It was remarkably fresh on television too.

AS   M'm. It was very difficult to do because it was never made for television. Suddenly to be in the studio alone, with no audience, and with all the pressures, was not so good. It was still fun to do, I suppose, but not the same as on the stage.

PB   When you appear in other people's plays, written-down plays, do you find them comparatively boring?

AS   No, not really. It depends on the script. What I do know, though, is I'm happiest when I'm furthest away from myself.

Patience Collier

I visited Patience Collier at her home in Kensington at two-thirty p.m. on Thursday 3 March. She had just opened in *Lent* by Michael Wilcox at the Lyric Studio Theatre, Hammersmith. At three-thirty when we'd finished, and I'd switched off my pocket-sized cassette-recorder, she said she was going to rest and was already getting nervous for that evening's performance. I had promised I would take no more than an hour of her time, and left at three-thirty-five, after having said goodbye to Alice, her eighty-four-year-old cook-housekeeper.

*

PC   I've discovered a new word. Pith. An actor or an actress should have inside them the pith of the part they are playing. Now, if you are a woman of many parts, and I suppose I think I am, it means that I can play a murderess, or a beauty, or a mousey little person in the village, and they will all have the pith that's inside me. I mean, they can have my nose and be a beauty, because the beauty is in my head. And that's not sentimental, you know. I think I look quite pretty as Mrs Blake, this woman I'm playing now. And it's strange that I can use the word "pretty" about myself with my phizog.

PB   Pretty, yet frail.

PC   Well I'm frail because my face is frail now.

PB   But you look frailer. Very pale.

PC   I don't put any make-up on. But what I do is, before I put

151

on my wig, I dust my face and neck with Johnson's Baby
Powder, and on my lips I put a non-colour colour, which
gives them a shape and prevents them from looking dry
and crinkled.

PB   How did you start?

PC   Well, you know this play is partly autobiographical, all
about Michael Wilcox's days at prep. school, and so I
said to him did he know this woman, and he said, yes she
was my grandmother, and I said, have you got a picture
of her anywhere, and he said, yes, and he brought it; and
she had a square face and looked like Flora Robson. She
also had soft, pretty, idiotic white hair and it was so
untidy always, he said, that the family used to go about
catching the kirby grips. I had to get this sort of person, a
mixture of softness and discipline, into me. Now, in the
photograph she was wearing a two-piece, made of navy-
blue and white foulard, a fashionable material of the
time, so I said to Christopher Fettes, who was going to
direct it, "I can't do this part unless you let Cosprops
dress me." He said, "We can't afford them and they
won't do us." I said, "Yes they will, they'll do me: let me
get on the telephone." So I rang John Bright and said,
"Look, John, I'm stuck; I don't want to do a part unless I
can have a navy-blue and white foulard two-piece and a
navy-blue plain hat. If you can find them, I can do this
part; I can't otherwise because anything else will be too
smart, too vulgar or whatever." The following Tuesday I
went to him, and he had it hanging there.

PB   You have to ask for a lot in the theatre, don't you?

PC   Oh yes. You have to. It's not like filming. There you don't
have to ask for anything. You see I don't like economising
in any way, and in films they don't. If they want a
diamond necklace they get a diamond necklace: they get
everything and money isn't considered. They get it
because the director wants it and tells them to get it.
Anyway, for this play I went as usual to Wig Creations,
and I said to David, "Don't *make* me a wig," and I always
say this, "find me an old wig out of a drawer which you

can clean up and re-front, but it must be soft enough to be on to . . . to be *in* to my head." And then I thought to myself, I know what shoes I've got to wear, and I got my great big brown-and-white shoe-bag filled with shoes which I'd stolen, over the years, from the RSC (but Peter Hall and Trevor Nunn knew about this), and I found these white summer shoes which are so uncomfortable that I thought I can't walk better for this part than in these shoes because they're so uncomfortable. I wear them for hurt. So I haven't got to think about how to walk. The walk is done. The stick is my mother-in-law's, which she left here.

PB   And the voice is yours, isn't it?

PC   Oh, absolutely. And also it's mine not trying to be old, because I don't believe old people sound old. But fear of making an "acting" noise with an upper-class accent, because it is quite upper class, made me too quiet to start with, and the director said, "You must be tougher," and somebody who came to see the first dress rehearsal said, "You need some more decibels: you're being too modest."

PB   Did you go louder?

PC   Oh yes. One decibel up.

PB   You're the only person I've talked to for this book who has just done a First Night. How did you feel?

PC   Unready. I'm still unready. You see I haven't studied this play as I usually do; I haven't done it nearly so thoroughly.

PB   Why?

PC   No time. I've been spoilt at the RSC and the National with eleven weeks or nine weeks for rehearsal, and that's what I like: to have time to find out what the author's attitude was when writing the play, what the person I was to play was like as a child, how she grew up to be the adult she's become. I suppose I did this most for *The Government Inspector*, when I was the Mayor's wife, that idiot; and when I thought about it I got this child into my head who went in for Butlin's Holiday Camps' baby

153

competitions; she was not particularly pretty, but had hair that was gold and sharp, with curls, and I could hear her mum and dad and her auntie and uncle all saying, "Oh, isn't our Annie loovely?" "Don't her hair shine?" Dreadful voices, a dreadful accent. She was that sort of little girl: harsh, but loved by all these people. So I said to Peter Hall, "Can I do this part with this sort of voice?" and he said, "Absolutely: you keep on with that dreadful Butlin child." And later, he said, "Now put it into the accent we're going to use," and this accent had no "t's" or "r's", so I said "Pi'usburg", not "Petersburg": that sort of thing. And I kept the child's voice and the child's laugh for a time, and later Peter Hall said, "Now, keep this timbre, but grow up into a harshness: throw away the child." And with that harshness came the shape of my neck, and my mouth; but this was a long study, you see. And that woman, mutton dressed as lamb, became an inevitability. That's how I like to work.

PB   You give the impression, because of the sort of actress you are and the sort of person you are, that once your performance is set, that's how it stays. Is that right?

PC   No of course not. For instance I've just been practising a little moment where I think I spell it out too much.

PB   So if you want to change anything, you work it out at home and put the revised version into your performance that night?

PC   Yes. And nobody'll know but me.

PB   But apart from that you wouldn't risk a change on the spur of the moment?

PC   Never, never, never. Such a thing could not possibly happen to me, ever, to the end of the world.

PB   You've done a lot of radio. How do you approach a part when it's the voice only that you can use?

PC   Well I like radio because I can do voices. When they did a feature programme with eight women they used Betty Hardy and me for the eight: bus conductresses, beggars, nannies in the park and ladies at the hairdressers. But acting for radio has taught me an enormous amount

154

about words, which I would never have known if I hadn't done it.

PB   Such as?

PC   Well it taught me about people's listenability.

PB   What does that mean?

PC   Well . . . if you lived with Alice you'd know she doesn't hear anything I say, however clearly I say it. I mean if I say, "Alice, I think today, the best thing to do is to buy a white loaf," she'll say, "M'm," and I know she hasn't heard because she's been looking out of the window, and then she'll say, "What did you say?" and I have to say it all over again and she'll say, "Oh yes. Right ho."

Now if you are on the radio, you say things with pauses behind them. You say: "Darling, when you go to the shops, get me a white loaf, will you?" and you do a tiny pause, before the word "white". And you whistle the "wh". And if you say, "Try not to make mistakes this morning," there's a funny thing behind an "m". There are things behind words, you see, which shouldn't be made big but should be there.

PB   Say your line is, "It's hot today," how far do you like to go into the feeling of heat, which perhaps you wouldn't bother to do if you could be seen?

PC   It depends what the heat is doing to you. It can be hurting you, relieving you, or tantalising you, and you put that in. There's no limit to what you can do with words.

PB   Do you write on your script?

PC   Write? I can't see the script. There's only one person who wrote more on her script that me and that was Edith Evans. She underlined all her own words in red, and every cue with green, and every cue-light with a green asterisk. I've always done those things too; I draw funny pictures like waves to remind me of how a line should be inflected. Not proper things, but things I know about. A mess. I do what suits me, when I want to. No rules. I love radio.

PB   You've hinted you like filming too.

PC   Oh films are wonderful because you can take three years to say, "How do you do," or "Come in!" Yes, I love filming.

PB   What is it that you like about it? Doing it in little bits?

PC   No: the fuss that is made of me. My ego is in a joy. First of all, for a close-up in a film which is important, you have the biggest, closest light on your face that can exist on earth without killing you. Then, everybody is attending to you, powdering, patting, combing, pinning, minding, not because they love you, but because they've got to do it. It's all the time they spend on you that I love: the wig-fitting and the make-up and the clothes.

     You see, at the age of eighteen months I experienced my first "audience reaction". I was sitting on my mother's drawing-room carpet with a white sheet thrown over it, and in front of me were spread currants, raisins and sultanas, and three jars; and my mother said, "Now, darling, try to separate those three things, the currants, raisins and sultanas." And I knew that my finger-tips were being watched by elderly ladies in furs and crêpe de Chine, and they said, "Isn't she sweet?" "Isn't she a clever little girl?" and "You've got a treasure, Eva." They were talking to my mother, but I remembered what they said, and then forgot. But years later, when I was in the revue, *Living for Pleasure*, at the Garrick Theatre, and I was doing my solo number, "I'm the lady who sits at the loo at the Ritz", dressed in pitch black, with all the lights on me, I remembered the little girl in white all over again. It was "audience reaction" which made me have to be an actress, I suppose.

PB   Which directors have influenced you most?

PC   Oh . . . I've worked with so many . . . but I suppose I can't imagine what life was like before Joan Littlewood.

PB   In what way?

PC   Well, she taught me things I never thought existed.

PB   Such as?

PC   Well, for instance, she asked me to play Mrs Gilchrist in her production of *The Hostage* in New York. In the week

156

before I flew out there I went to Stratford East and learned all the songs and dances; and when I arrived in New York, I went to a fiendish rehearsal room off Broadway, and Joan was there, and I walked in, and although we hadn't seen each other for years she didn't say good morning, she didn't say thank you for coming, she didn't say hello; she said, "Patience," and I walked over to where she was talking to other people. "Patience. Now. I've watched you for many years and as far as I can see you get a lot of things right. Your diction's very good, your accents are very good, your walks are very good, your clothes are miraculous, you always know your lines, you're always on time and you're a hard worker. Have you ever thought about love?" And I said, "What do you mean?" and she said, "Have you ever thought about the audience loving you and you loving them?" I said, "Well, no, never," and she said, "Well, this is what you've got to learn this time. I'll teach you."

PB   And did she?

PC   Oh yes. I couldn't do my present part without Joan. Without the years-ago Joan. In *The Hostage* I had to sing a solo in a spotlight, and she said, "Now, don't have a singing lesson. I'm sure you've got a pretty voice." And she said, "Look how you're standing! Your bottom's out at the back: pull it in, stick out your breasts and give yourself to the audience. Don't beg, don't lean forward, let them come to you, welcome them with open arms, and sing,

> 'Only a box of matches
> Across the Irish sea.' "

And she said, "When you do this, the audience in the front stalls will be like beds of asparagus. You'll feel like a young virgin, teasing them away. And you'll sing like a genius." And I did. I had never before been on a stage with no nerves, no fears, no inhibitions. I loved it. I loved getting ready. I loved the warm-ups, I loved the character, I loved the audiences in New York. Joan Littlewood taught me to reach. To reach people. Or rather, to bring the audience to me.

Roger Rees

I interviewed Roger Rees on Tuesday 8 March. He was then well into a long run of *The Real Thing* by Tom Stoppard, at the Strand Theatre.

*

RR   Oh, I panicked a great deal during the rehearsals for *The Real Thing*. Peter Wood expected a lot and he was quite right; but the rehearsal period was very short – only three weeks – and every day words were being changed, speeches were being changed, or put in different places, and I felt I was just being pushed along; and all the time I was trying to find this man, this writer, who starts very eccentrically, being rude to everyone, and then becomes a sort of redeemable creature that you want to hug, someone who is not brittle any more.

PB   Do you often panic?

RR   It's a feeling that's been with me for a long time. I was a choirboy at our local church in Balham and we were going to sing at Southwark Cathedral, and I was going to sing a solo: "Once in Royal David's City". And after school that day, I went, and got as far as the door, and I didn't go in. I walked off down the road. Someone else had to sing it. Just because I was scared. I walked and walked. There's still a great strain in what I do and I think that's probably why it comes out in such a nervous way. I even find walking about difficult; and sometimes when I have a long speech I feel embarrassed, so I do it as quickly as I can just to get it over with and let somebody else do something. I think that's why I act so quickly. I am embracing a fear. When I was a boy I found it hard to throw myself wholeheartedly into things because I was even then an observer. I watched. And I find now that if I have to do anything extremely physical or frightening on the stage, I am able to stand completely outside myself, really look at myself, almost see myself from the back of the auditorium. And I hate it. It makes me feel po-faced and unadventurous; and that's why sometimes I do physical things which are quite wrong, quite embarrassing; but I have to do them just for *my* sake. It's me fighting against myself, and I think that's what acting is about. I don't want just to be safe, or just to be careful. I'm prepared to be embarrassing. David Threlfall, who was Smike in *Nicholas Nickleby*, said to me, "You do light-bulb acting."

PB   What did he mean?

RR   Well, that I go, "Whish, whish, whow," you know, putting in the light bulb, "whow", it's the twist of the hand, the added thing. It's like jumping or dancing. If I elect to put my hands in my pockets I thrust them in like this, or if I sit I hunch myself up in the chair or something like that. It's an elaboration, a decoration on top.

PB   Do you do these things in order to be interesting?

RR   I don't think just to say the words is exciting. So, yes I do.

PB   John Hurt told me this morning that he's sick of naturalism. "We are entertainers, after all," he said, "and we need a sort of heightened naturalism." Do you agree?

RR   Yes. Yes I do.

PB   You do act very physically . . .

RR   Yes I know.

PB   . . . for example at the end of each part of *Nicholas Nickleby*: there was a great yearning and love for Smike at the end of Part I and for the crippled boy at the end of Part II, and you expressed these feelings with yearning

159

movements. Not like the movements which a dancer might make, but going that way.

RR Yes. That's what I'm afraid of. I don't want it to look like a dance. And yet I feel words need assistance. I feel the story-telling needs assistance. When Smike said to Nicholas, "You are my home," I turned away from him and looked up at the sky. Thelma Whiteley said to me, "Why do you do that? Do you need it?" And I thought I did . . . I could explain it as a sort of Christian thing, but that was the moment I made the decision to take him with me.

PB Yes, those sort of things are rather your trademark, aren't they? Those and speed.

RR I suppose so. When I was Roderigo and Emrys James was Iago my mother said, "That Emrys James, he wasn't jerky, was he?" But I can't really call it jerky any more because I've chosen to use the febrile side of my nature. I *am* influenced by dance. Or perhaps by rhythms – rhythms of the body, rhythms of speech. A sort of musicality. I think the first thing I caught when I read *The Real Thing* was the rhythms of Tom Stoppard's jokes. I think for any part which I have I should use everything I can: so I include everything. Maybe it's too like a bargain basement in the end. In *The Real Thing* I like to try to express Henry's unhappiness very physically and I move about all over the place. I guess other actors wouldn't do that; they would do it just with the words. But I can't keep my hands in my pockets, as it were. I suppose a lot of it is wanting to be . . .

PB . . . Wanting to be exciting?

RR . . . because I want the audience to feel a kind of excitement. I love it, when I'm in the audience, to feel actors' passions coming across to me. So when I'm acting I feel I should just go out there and . . . I mean plays are written about special days, aren't they, not about any old day?

PB Do your performances become very set?

RR Not at all. I like to vary. As long as the intentions remain

160

the same. My understudy said to me the other day, with great surprise: "Someone told me you change things in performance." But I like to. I'd be crazy by now if I didn't. Stoppard is quite hard to do, and requires a great deal of physical energy. It's like digging a hole in the road every night.

PB   Are you sometimes afraid of becoming too mannered?

RR   Yes. I have to watch it. I don't like watching mannered actors, because I can't listen to them; and the only way to act really well is to tell a story properly. I find it boring and unsatisfying when the story isn't told, when people occlude what the part they are playing wants to say by doing things which other people have applauded them for over the years, by merely parading themselves and their mannerisms.

PB   Do you work out your performances at home?

RR   Not at all. Things happen at rehearsal and I either accept them or reject them. If ever I work out something at home I usually don't have the gall to suggest it. And sometimes if I think in advance of something funny I'd like to say, and wait for an opportunity to say it, it never comes out right. I can always say it on the stairs afterwards but then it's too late. Anything I prepare becomes arid. And anyway, preparation like that suggests there's something perfect about what you want to achieve, and I don't think it's like that: it's more like a plant, or a piece of fruit which grows and you say, oh this is ready to eat now, but as you say that it can go off as well. I think it's death when you say to yourself, oh yes, isn't that a great moment? And you try to reproduce it. I mean, our job *is* to reproduce, isn't it? But you don't feel the same every night, the audience is different every night, so you can only approximate.

PB   You've just played Oswald in *Ghosts* on the radio, haven't you? How do you react to last-minute notes from the director?

RR   I'm a very obedient soul, I think, and I rather like last-minute notes.

161

PB Do you like the mechanics of radio?

RR Oh yes. It becomes, "Who can turn the page best?" doesn't it? Sian Phillips was very clever at it, and she'd keep her script in front of me, while I was turning my page over my shoulder, so I could go on reading. I mean it's not natural to talk with a big piece of paper in your hand, and your neck craned round, is it? And you're talking to a piece of machinery: you're not talking to the person you love or hate. It's all ludicrous really, so you might as well join in. I think my favourite is walking out of a door backwards so you can still speak to the microphone.

PB Somebody described you as one of our most watchable actors. Do you regard that as a compliment?

RR I'm not sure. I just feel I should go as far as possible and yet be as rivetingly real as possible. That's what I feel

Prunella Scales

I interviewed Prunella Scales at her home just by Wandsworth Common on Monday 27 June. She had been in Australia, touring her programme about Queen Victoria, when I was doing the foregoing series of interviews.

*

PS   I always hope to start with what I can only call a strong feeling for the part. I never know where that feeling comes from. It can come from a person I know or have seen in the street, or from a character I've read about, or even from (and this will seem heresy to some actors) somebody else's performance.

PB   When you read a play for the first time, do you read any of it aloud?

PS   No, never. I make myself read the whole play in silence. It was one of the things dinned into us at the Old Vic School: "An actor's first duty is to the play." After reading the play I always want to talk to the author. Often an author can tell you where a character was born, and when, what her childhood was like, even what she looks or sounds like. Often authors can't or won't talk, of course, either because they believe in letting you flounder, or because they're dead.

Quite often, usually after a week or so of rehearsals, I write out a rough list of dates in the character's life: date of birth, date of leaving school, date of marriage, date of

163

parents' death, etc. . . . . Then I can work out what songs they've heard in their childhood, what world events they've lived through, what books they are likely to have read, what fashions they've seen, what dances they've learnt, all of which can be helpful from time to time.

PB   The voice of a part is very important to you, isn't it?

PS   I'm never happy until I have found the physical individuality of a part, which includes the voice, I suppose. I've got quite a useful, strong and variable voice, and quite a good ear both for regional dialects and for mannerisms of speech, which is probably just as well because I'm not very versatile physically: I'm quite short and I haven't got a very useful face. A critic very kindly wrote of me once that the six parts I played in one play were nicely differentiated vocally, but that I couldn't change my face, which was that of a worried hamster.

PB   Do you do homework?

PS   Yes, a lot. Perhaps, because I've got a fairly demanding family, I don't work as hard as I should. But, yes, a lot. My eldest son once said to me, "Mummy, you don't understand about homework," and I'm afraid I hit him. Quite hard.

PB   Someone said of your performance in Simon Gray's *Quartermaine's Terms* that you managed to be very real and yet comment on the character at the same time. I thought the same about you in Michael Frayn's *Make and Break*. Are you aware of this commenting?

PS   Oh yes. I think this is partly because both those plays were by authors who write with a very delicate balance between, for want of better words, drama and comedy. And therefore there was an implied comment on every character in them. As there is, too, in the plays of Chekhov: he has an oblique view of his characters, he comments on life through them; and I suppose it is the actor's task to realise this: to be truthful, of course, but not entirely subjective.

PB   This whole business of comedy, now. You are notably successful at it. What skills do you rely on?

164

PS   I think a sense of timing, a sense of comedy, a sense of what is funny about a part, are gifts from God. God or whoever. But you can help them along in various ways, for example with rhythm or with different dynamics. To put it no higher, I think you can get laughs in the theatre by tickling the audience's ears, by surprising them: I mean loud and soft and fast and slow, really. Music can be funny in the same way.

PB   By "rhythm", do you mean keeping the momentum of a line going, right through to the final word?

PS   I think it's more a question of phrasing. Phrasing and stress. I learned about this through John Gielgud. Janet Suzman told me once that when she was going to play Saint Joan, Gielgud said to her, "Don't forget that in Shaw, there's only one main stress in every sentence." And I've found that true not only of Shaw but of almost everything: of colloquial speech, of mannered speech in Restoration comedy, of situation comedy on television. Rationing the stresses like this isn't dull, it's the reverse of dull: it makes speech rapid, shifting and varied, and is very good for comedy. All the best comedians I know – for example Richard Briers, John Cleese, Ronnie Barker – have an enormous feeling for rapid speech, which is not so much their skill in diction, although heaven knows that is considerable, as their feeling for stresses and how few they need to use.

PB   Do you enjoy doing situation comedies?

PS   Oh yes, except that the half-hour episodes come round so quickly, once a week; and in *Fawlty Towers* I never felt ready to do it every Sunday night. But John Cleese gave me great courage. It was rather like working with a live machine-gun which you try to keep pointing away from you. But you feel you've got something to bash against and that's very comforting. Leonard Rossiter's the same.

PB   Earlier in this book, I've tried doing stresses for a bit of King Magnus's long speech, and I found there was often more than one in each sentence.

PS   Oh, I think Gielgud meant that there should be only one *main* stress. I suppose the usual thing is to go for the noun. Like I've just done: "I suppose the usual thing is to go for the <u>noun</u>." If you stress something that's not a noun you can get character and eccentricity. For example, if I said, "the <u>usual</u> thing is to go for the noun," I might sound like an intense actress talking about her work. Or you might stress every single word. I mean you <u>might/stress/ every/single/word</u>. And that, too, tells you something about the character. And if you stress prepositions and conjunctions you will sound like a newsreader or a sports reporter:

> To be <u>or</u> not to be – that <u>is</u> the question;
> Whether 'tis nobler <u>in</u> the mind to suffer
> The slings <u>and</u> arrows <u>of</u> outrageous fortune,
> Or to take arms <u>against</u> a sea <u>of</u> troubles,
> And <u>by</u> opposing end them?

PB   I wonder why so many of us want to stress too many words, and speak syllabically? Is it a relic of the English classic tradition?

PS   I suspect rather it's because we don't listen properly to the nuances of everyday speech. But even with classical texts it's easy to overstress. I've found through poetry readings, for instance, that it's usually better to let subordinate clauses ride without stress or emphasis.

PB   For example?

PS   Well . . . Shakespeare's sonnet 23:

> As an unperfect actor on the stage
> Who with his fear is put besides his part,
> Or some fierce thing replete with too much rage,
> Whose strength's abundance weakens his own
>   heart;
> So I, for fear of trust, forget to say
> The perfect ceremony of love's rite,
> And in mine own love's strength seem to decay,
> O'ercharg'd with burthen of mine own love's might.

The main sentence there is:

> I . . . forget to say . . . love's rite,
> And in mine own love's strength seem to decay.

And I think it's easy to betray the real sense of the sonnet unless you put brackets round the rest of it and just let the words themselves do the work for you. Without over-colouring.

PB   In the theatre, does playing out-front present any problems for you?

PS   Not where I have to talk to the audience directly – asides and so on. But in "private" parts I think I'm inclined to refuse my eyes to the audience. I have to *make* myself look out. In a realistic play you have to know what you're supposed to be looking at, which is not the front row of the upper circle: you're looking through a window, or over the countryside, or at the fourth wall of the room. If you take care of that it can help you to stop feeling frightened of the audience.

PB   Do you enjoy the repetition of a long run?

PS   Yes.

PB   Do you ever get carried away and do different moves and things?

PS   No. That is, I'd never change something that affected other actors without discussing it first. But sometimes, especially in *Queen Victoria*, a great deal of which is monologue, when there's a very sympathetic audience or for whatever reason, I feel I begin to fly. We none of us know why this happens, do we? But new things which happen on those nights can be incorporated into future performances.

PB   Do you ever fly when you teach as well?

PS   Oh, I don't know, but I love it. I learn so much. Just now I'm getting the chance to try a number of things at the Actors' Centre – I'm doing a new workshop tomorrow, on acting for radio. I think the thing which sorted me out, for both acting and teaching, and any directing which I occasionally do, was working with Uta Hagen in New York many, many years ago; and still I constantly refer to her book, *Respect for Acting*. She evolved a sort of grammar of acting, which is not dry, which is nothing but truth and common sense. Harold Pinter says, "Acting is common sense." John Cleese says, "Acting is common sense." And John Cleese read law at Cambridge, Jonathan Miller is a doctor, Chekhov was a doctor. All this has stopped my fear that I might be too analytical: it is manifestly untrue that a cerebral approach necessarily dries up emotion or spontaneous feeling. Uta Hagen's method of acting, which is out of Stanislavski, by various American "method" directors, is simple and sensible.

PB   Can you summarise?

PS   She says the first question you must ask yourself is, "Who am I?" The second question is, "What do I want?" The third is, "What is the obstacle?" And then, "What do I do to overcome the obstacle and achieve what I want?" Then there are various other things like, "What are the conditions? Is it hot or cold? What sort of state am I in? How do the other people affect what I do?"

PB   An example?

PS   Well. A trivial example. I'm an aide-de-camp and I have to come in and say to the commanding officer, "Good morning, sir. Here is the report from Major Smith. In it you will see that he estimates the enemy will be with us at approximately eight hundred hours tomorrow morning." Now. Who am I? I am Lieutenant Bloggs. Which probably means that I have been trained to keep a stiff upper lip and not to show emotion of any kind. What do I want? (At Uta's classes you're taught always to look for a *verb*, never for a quality or an emotion.) I may want to do my duty, or to avoid showing fear, or perhaps I want my breakfast. What is the obstacle? Perhaps the CO is in a bad mood, perhaps I'm frightened of him or of the impending attack. So what do I do? I probably come in and mutter the line as quickly as possible and get out. It'll be over in two seconds but it will be true and at least it won't be over-acted. If you *try* for an emotion, try to feel, it's a sure way of cutting off emotion altogether. Acting is doing.

     When I was a student at the Old Vic School, Glen Byam Shaw was one of the directors, and although he taught me a lot he had an extreme suspicion of anything which he thought was intellectuality; and I got myself lumbered, partly, I expect, because I wore glasses in those days and was fearfully earnest . . . well . . . he said, "Oh Prunella, you tackle your work like a piece of arithmetic," and I was very frightened of this. But what I learned from Uta is that there is absolutely no reason why you shouldn't bring every faculty you have in life to bear on your work. It will open up channels, particularly emotional channels. In *Quartermaine's Terms* I couldn't stop crying . . .

How Do I Work On A Part? ~

This is nothing more than a postscript to the previous chapter, which I enjoyed compiling, noticing especially how those I interviewed resorted to images and analogies: Judi Dench's "green Swiss hill", and "signposts", Alex McCowen's "as ifs", Edward Petherbridge's "prize garden", Anna Massey's "frozen, blocked drains", Alison Steadman's "first mark on the canvas" and Roger Rees's "digging a hole in the road".

*

Here's another. In 1958 I moved into a new flat. It was the first time I had more than one room, and my own front door, which I could close. I was in *Roar Like A Dove* at the Phoenix Theatre and had been moaning to Ewan Roberts, who was also in it, about the dreadful basement I had been living in for some time. "Well, look in the *Evening Standard*," he said, irritated, "and do something." So we looked together, and saw that there was a "top-floor flat, 32 Bernard Street, WC1. Rent £3.5s a week, entire contents for sale £650".

"There you are," said Ewan, "it's an omen." The part I had in the play was called Bernard. "Go for that one."

"But I haven't got £650. I've only got £300. In the Halifax."

"Go and see it. If it's perfect you can raise the rest of the money somehow."

I went; it *was* perfect: two rooms, kitchen and bath, nicely furnished; what's more it was only ten minutes' walk from the theatre, and five minutes from RADA, where I was then taking a lot of classes. Mr and Mrs Ring, who were leaving it, liked me, and said I could have the contents for £600. "Done," I said, and rang my father to ask for a loan of £300.

*

And it's here that my analogy begins. Moving into a new flat, I thought, especially into a furnished flat, is like taking on a new part. First of all you see it. And if you like it and the terms are right, you accept it. And that is, as Judi Dench said, the most thrilling part of all. You are on the hill.

Then you go back to your old place and think about the new one. And start worrying. Because, actually, you did not look carefully enough: you let your enthusiasm carry you away. When you come to think of it, there are snags: will you be able to put up with the floors which, you happened to notice but didn't bother about at the time, creaked? Do you really like all that cane furniture? Won't it have to be replaced? Worst of all, what you had absolutely not considered, there is no room in the flat for your baby-grand piano. They'd never get it up the stairs: and because the floor creaks and slopes a bit, and because it wouldn't be fair on the person in the flat underneath, you'll have to sell it. Damn! And where the hell is all the furniture you've already got, which you're definitely not going to sell, going to go? You'll sell the piano because you have to, but everything else matters far too much. There's nothing else for it, you'll have to go back and have another look.

They are nice and let you wander around on your own. "As long as you like," they say, "and we'll keep out of your way; but if you want to ask us anything, please don't hesitate. We know what it's like, moving into a new place. We're having to do the same, of course. So we're all in the same boat, aren't we?" You all laugh, and feel better for it. After all, there is no rush: you don't have to make instant decisions about what you'll get rid of and where your furniture will go. In fact it would be better to wait until you move in, and then see. You'll be able to play around with it then, and move things. And the cane furniture isn't quite as bad as you'd thought: when you've put some of

171

your own ornaments on it, and books and things, it could look quite nice.

So you wait, more hopefully, with less panic; and little ideas occur to you from time to time. There's suddenly rather a lot to do, too, in preparation: there's selling the piano, and arranging for a van to take your things, and telling everybody what your new address and telephone number are going to be.

Moving-in day arrives. You hadn't anticipated how tiring it would be, humping the furniture into the van at the old place and, worse, humping it out at the new, with all those stairs to climb. Up and down. Up and down. Eventually the van-man leaves, you close the front door, heave a sigh of relief, look round and see nothing but chaos.

"Christ," you think, "what have I done? Look at it! It's dreadful. And I've got to go out soon and do some work. I can't leave it like this." And you sit down and mope and feel full of despair. You go into the kitchen and try to find their kettle, which is not at all like the one you're used to, and far more awkward because it's got a cover over where you pour the water in, and it's very stiff, this cover, and you'll have to do something about that, but not now: you're too tired. "Sit down," you say to yourself, "have a cup of tea, and don't do any more work on the flat until tomorrow."

When you come back that night, you think, "It's not home. It's not home at all. I hate it. I wish I'd never come here. I wish I'd stayed in that basement which was not so bad after all. At least there weren't all these bloody stairs to climb. I mean, I know there was dry rot there and it was dreadful. But at least I wouldn't have had to endure all this." You have a drink, feel a bit better, go to bed, and just before you go to sleep you think, "Well, I'll work on it tomorrow. And I'll try not to rush it. I don't want to make mistakes. I want to do it properly. So if I get irritated, I'll stop. I'm glad I stopped today when I did. That little sit-down was a good idea."

The following morning you work out a scheme. Room by room. There's very little to do in the bathroom, so that can take care of itself. The kitchen must be done, and must be done this morning. "I must put things away, and remember where I've put them," you say aloud to yourself, with emphasis. "Be sensible," you instruct yourself. Tins there, cups and saucers there, pans there. Sort it out. And while you're about it you might as well sort out the types of tin, so they're not muddled. Soup tins there, Heinz baked beans there, and fish and meat there. This will probably take all morning and then you can clean the floor. Scour it. It's filthy. No point in having tidy cupboards and a filthy floor.

That's enough for today. Tomorrow you'll do the same in the bedroom. You go out to work and come back and it still doesn't feel like home. But there's something to look at at last: there's the kitchen. So you pour yourself a drink and go and sit in the kitchen and feel pleased with yourself. "It's good, what I did today," you think. And you stare at it.

The following day you have a first go at the bedroom, and it's all beginning to look a bit more ship-shape. And, more importantly, you're beginning to know it. The kitchen's getting good. You could invite people to look at the kitchen. (Only the kitchen, though, so you won't have people there yet.) But you've spent some hours there now, and you've worked on it, and it's not home yet but it's certainly not depressing any more and there's light at the end of the tunnel.

The only thing is, what are you going to do about the sitting-room? You don't mind the floor, that's minor and you can put up with it; but what are you going to do about the furniture you brought, and the furniture that was there? You start by humping it around all over again, and it's quite fun. Yes: for the first time it's fun. Some arrangements are better than others and eventually you make a few decisions. The sofa must be here because the speakers must be there and if the speakers are there, the turntable must be here. Right. Let's have a look. There's a table too many, one of those you brought. Right. Get rid of it.

What you certainly will get rid of are their ornaments, their little things which you positively do not like. They do not suit you. But in addition to getting rid of things there are one or two new things you will have to buy. A standard lamp would look very nice in that corner, and you need another chair.

173

So the following day you go out shopping. It's a relief to be outside, and you've decided to take your time. You look in the windows of several furniture shops, but go in only if it looks a likely place. You talk to the assistants and state your requirements and if they come up with something approximating what you want you say you will think about it. What you're really hoping for is that they will have something better than you had anticipated: more useful, prettier or whatever. And then, if it doesn't cost you too much, you say you'll have it. You take it home, and it *is* home now and, oh yes, it fits.

But now you've cleaned it all and know where everything is, it looks a bit bare. The walls are bare. You haven't put any pictures up yet. It isn't ornamented enough. So you play around with the few you've got, decide where to put them, and hang them up.

It's getting good now. As good as you, the flat itself, your things and their things and what you manage to buy, can make it. Now you can show it to people. You start with a few friends; and their presence makes you a bit self-conscious about it and you notice all kinds of little details which aren't quite right yet. You don't point them out, of course, but you see the flaws more readily than the successes. Nevertheless they all exclaim about it and congratulate you. Later in the evening when they've had a bit to drink, they volunteer a suggestion or two which, because you're in such a good mood, you accept with pleasure, saying you'll do something about them the following day.

At last you give a house-warming party. Your flat is teeming with people and the party is a success. Well, if you were to be honest, a qualified success. It was a bit too hot, and you were on edge and a bit too nervous to enjoy it properly. You were too anxious for it to be a success. When you give another party it will be better because you'll be more relaxed about it. You certainly learned from the first one: you noticed the flat felt very different with a lot of people there.

And so the weeks pass, and you live there. You make little improvements from time to time as they occur to you. Nothing drastic. Nothing too big. Of course, sometimes things go wrong and you have to work at them: the fridge breaks down and has to be seen to – you have to get somebody in to do that. Eventually you get a new kettle. But the pressure is off now and these little bits of work and little improvements are no hardship.

Perhaps the worst that can happen, as the weeks become months and the months become years, is that you will get bored with it and not look at it any more, not take any more pride in it. So perhaps then you might buy something new, a new picture, something special: something which will make you look at everything all over again, and bring life back into the place.

*

I thought of this analogy the day after I had moved into my flat at 32 Bernard Street, and I couldn't wait to get to my next class at RADA to tell them about it. "Yesterday I moved into a new flat, and I thought, moving into a new flat, especially this particular flat, which is fully furnished, is rather like taking on a new part . . ."

This Is What Happens When You Go Filming ~

"I think," said Edward Woodward loudly, when we were sitting in a caravan in the middle of a field, "that all drama students should be made to sit in a caravan in the middle of a field for a WEEK," (he is a born raconteur and suddenly hits words with an unexpected fury) "for a whole WEEK, and never, ever be used. Not once. Oh, they'll be made up and dressed, and the boys will have little white tissues tucked into their necks to protect their collars from their make-up and the girls will sit carefully so as not to crease their skirts too much. And everybody will look in the mirror from time to time to see what they look like and if their hair's still all right. They will trudge across the field to queue for their meals outside the location caterers' vehicle, and carry them (soup in plastic beakers and roast chicken and stewed vegetables on a cardboard plate) back to the caravan. They will eke out the meal for as long as they can; and some fool will volunteer to wallow back to the location caterers with all the dirties, and return with requested fruit, cheese and biscuits, coffees and teas. At the end of the lunch-break they will be called to the make-up bus for a check-up, and be told by the second assistant that, hopefully, if the damp weather holds, they'll be needed for a line-up in about two hours. After four hours have passed the second assistant calls again with a few sheets of new dialogue and panics them all by saying, 'The director felt this scene wasn't quite right, so here's an amended version. We hope to be able to shoot it in

176

about half an hour.' Two hours later he calls again to say it's a wrap for the day. He gives them their call-sheets for tomorrow, which say they are to be made up and dressed by eight o'clock sharp. But they never, ever, get used."

*

That's the trouble with filming: it's either all or nothing. Unless you have a leading role it's mostly nothing. But during the nothing you have to be ready for the all. During the nothing, when an hour feels as long as a day, everyone chats. The actors huddle together and swap stories and roar with laughter, or go very quiet when they start moaning about the lack of organisation, or why were they called so early when everyone knew there was no hope of their being used, and why is this particular bunch of location caterers the worst they've ever come across? Actresses like to slink off occasionally to the make-up bus and chat to the make-up girls, who, after the early-morning rush, are in their own nothing for most of the rest of the day.

I like the huddled groups of talking, in fields or in caravans, especially when the talk is funny. Or a moan. You have to say things from time to time, or you'd go mad.

At least it keeps you from brooding and from going over the lines of your next scene so often that you don't know what they mean any more. I was in a film once – *Patton (Blood and Guts)* – in which I had one line only; and I had to wait in Spain for nearly three months to say it. The line was to Michael Bates (General Montgomery) and I had to go up to him, salute and say, "Sir, Patton's taken Palermo." I heaved myself along a Spanish beach for days on end, wondering which word to emphasise: "Sir, Patton's <u>taken</u> Palermo" (meaning "we didn't want him to, did we? And now he's gone and done it"); "Sir, Patton's taken <u>Palermo</u>" (meaning, "he's got as far as that," or "it's the wrong place"); and even, "Sir, <u>Patton's</u> taken Palermo" (meaning, "instead of you, sir. It should have been you.") When the day finally arrived I discovered I had to be driven up in a jeep, over very rough ground. Well, in filming, everyone shows off, and the driver wanted to show how fast he could drive the jeep and stop it on its stop-marks – bits of batten nailed into the grass. He drove so fast that I leapt into the air and banged my head on an iron bar above me which was there for generals to hold if they had to stand up and inspect troops. My cap came off and fell on to the ground as I got out, so I picked it up because I knew it would be wrong to salute without wearing it, arrived at Montgomery's desk in the sun and, by now dazed, said plainly, with no emphasis at all, "Sir, Patton's taken Palermo."

The director said, "Cut," complimented me on the delivery of my line, but told me off for picking up my cap and, thank heavens, told the driver off for driving so fast and said, "We'll go again." Take two. Perfect. "Right, print it." And that was that. The only thing was, the whole scene was cut from the eventual film.

*

However, in spite of all the enjoyments of perpetual talking – and people in films never stop – I think my favourite, and probably best, filming days have been those when, during prolonged nothings, I have been able to go off somewhere on my own and get on with something. Reading, usually, or writing. Why waste the time? (Someone said, "The art of filming is to be there, but not to be seen to be there until you are wanted." Someone else said, putting it slightly differently, "The art of filming is never to be noticeably absent or needlessly present.") It's good, this, because you don't waste your energy either; and if you really concentrate on something else you get into that mood of concentration which is the best thing in the world for acting.

Especially for acting in films. Because, when it comes to the "all", this is what happens; or at least this is what happened on my first day in *Champions*, and as it was a very typical filming day, I'll go through the sequence of events as I can now remember them. We were in the disused Wimbledon Hospital on the south side of the Common. A ward had been refurbished. John Hurt, as Bob Champion, the jockey, was in a bed by a window, and there were extras in all the other beds: some of them had had to have their heads shaved on account of the treatment for cancer they were supposed to be undergoing. The

178

scene was about Edward Woodward, as the trainer of the horse Aldaniti, and me, as its owner, visiting John to see how he was. Edward and I were called into the ward to rehearse it, and John Irvin, the director, came over to us and said, "Welcome." They'd just finished the previous scene of the day's schedule and everything was being moved. "Chippies" were banging away, taking out battens which had been fastened to the floor and removing the miniature railway track which had been laid so that the camera could be wheeled smoothly. "Sparks" were removing heavy, cumbersome lamps, and everyone was talking.

"Can I have quiet, please," the director said to the first assistant.

"Quiet everybody, please!" bawled the first assistant, who is the sergeant-major of the unit, and who organises everything and never stops working and planning. "I said QUIET. We want to REHEARSE this scene."

"Thank you," said the director quietly. And then he turned to us and said, "Now, let's go through this scene gently and see what happens. We'll do it several times." After the commotion, the hush was very comforting. The director wanted us to feel relaxed and easy, especially as it was our first day. "Edward and Peter," he continued, even more quietly, everyone hanging on his every word by now, "you come through the door, say good afternoon or something to a nurse we'll have leaving the ward as you come in, look round for John's bed, see him, and then approach him and . . . er . . . well, let's see what happens."

We tried it, got to the bed, and started the dialogue.

"Er," said the director. "I think it would be better to start the dialogue before you get to the bed and, Edward, you come this side of Peter and go closer to John; and, Peter, you could perhaps get a chair from the middle of the room, there by that table with the flowers on it, and bring it up to the bed and sit."

So we started again and this time got through the scene. Two and half pages of dialogue.

"Er . . ." said the director, trying to make it natural for us but realising he had to shoot it, and trying to work out camera-angles and something of the later editing: the cuts from shots

179

including the three of us to two-shots and singles, ". . . Peter, don't go for the chair and don't sit down; and we've got to get some glasses for the champagne somehow, haven't we? There'll be only one tooth-glass on John's bedside table, so, Peter, perhaps when it comes to the champagne bit you could go and get another one from the middle table. Yes, go then. Edward: is there time to open the champagne, do you think?"

"Well, I doubt it. I think it'll have to be prepared a bit. So that I just have to do the final twist of the wire or something."

"Let's try it again."

And we did. And then the director had a long muttered conversation, which we didn't listen to, with the lighting-cameraman and the camera-operator.

The director came back to us. "Yes," he said. "Good. Getting there. But Peter: the going for the glass is very good; but when you've got it, could you bring it closer to Edward while he pours, and then stroll round to the foot of the bed and stay there till the end of the scene. Let's just try that bit."

We did. "That better?" the director turned to the lighting-cameraman.

"Much."

"Right. Let's try the whole scene through once more." And afterwards he said, "Good. You can relax now John, Edward and Peter, and for the first shot we'll start on John talking to the nurse, then the camera will swing round following the nurse to the door and you come in, look round and see John. That's as far as we'll go."

"Right. Relax the artistes," said Bert, the first assistant – gradually you learn the names – "and, boys, carry on working. Any idea how long, Ronnie?" This to the lighting-cameraman, Ronnie Taylor, who did *Gandhi*.

"Ooh . . . well, with the camera swinging around we'll see most of the ward . . . ooh . . . an hour and a half, I should think."

"We'll be ready for you, gentlemen, in an hour and a half. Approximately," guffawed Bert, who has a voice to drown all others. "Stand-ins, please!"

We strolled away, talked for a while, realising there was a lot of time to kill, then peeled off to have a look at ourselves in

180

mirrors and go through the words a bit. All sorts of little decisions had to be made, too, about clothes and hair. For continuity. I think people in films often look too neat, too prepared, as though their hair has just been combed and brushed, and make-up newly applied, even after a fairly rough night or a bar-room brawl or a long trek through the mountains. This is partly because there's a department for everything, and each of them wants to display itself as efficient and good: so "hair" comes up and does it for you, "make-up" comes up and dabs you or slaps you around with a perfumed wet flannel when you're getting hot, and "wardrobe" comes up and brushes you down. But it's also partly because untidiness is harder to keep the same. We knew that the scene we were about to do would take the rest of the day. So if your hair is untidy, it has to be untidy in exactly the same way all day. If you have an untidy pocket handkerchief, just flung into your top pocket, it has to be pinned like that, very carefully, because the scene on the screen will last only about a minute and a half; and if it sinks in that time from a flamboyant billow to being hidden entirely in the pocket, and then suddenly bobs up again because someone has noticed, it will look silly. For the same reason ties, which can so easily slip, tend to be tied right into the collar, and trousers and skirts kept neatly pressed.

In the pause now I decided how I could keep my clothes right for continuity, by knowing how each little bit was going to be. My dark blue sweater covered the belt of my trousers by about two inches, and I decided to leave the top two buttons of my green quilted jacket undone, and the bottom one as well. This may seem unnecessarily fussy especially as there is always a continuity girl on hand to notice these things. But it's a nicer feeling if you get it right yourself, and anyway, she can't notice everything, especially when there's little rehearsal.

A year or two before this I had been in another film with Edward Woodward, and in one scene we had had to talk to each other across a dining-table, eating the while. I wouldn't let the director shoot the master (the master is the whole scene, shot usually from one all-seeing angle, showing most of the characters most of the time) until I had worked out what I was going to

181

do with the food: on which line I knived a potato on to my fork, when I lifted it to my mouth and when I ate it. I wanted to know what I ate, in what amounts, and when, because the master-shot was going to be followed by two two-shots: Edward over my shoulder and me over his, and two singles: Edward alone and me alone.

Edward said, "I'm surprised you fuss so: there's a girl to do all that."

"Well . . ." I said.

And I was glad I had fussed, because the closer shots were sure. Poor Edward had to do take after take of his close shots. "No Edward," said the girl, "I'm *sure* you had meat and carrots on your fork and put them in your mouth on that line."

"Yes," said the director, compassionately, "it's worth going again, Edward: I know it's tedious, but when I'm editing I'll probably want to use the master for the bit where you put peas and potatoes in your mouth, and follow it with a cut to you, and if you've suddenly got a whole heap of meat on your fork and cram that in too, I won't be able to use it."

Oh, I did want to say to Edward, "Told you so," but I refrained: he'd have laughed, I know, but perhaps not straightaway.

*

So when I'd thought about those things and had gone over in my mind the moves the director had given me, to be sure I could do them and feel comfortable with them, I tried to think all over again of the content of the scene. Let's see, I thought, Edward and I have driven up, perhaps had a vodka and tonic and a little lunch in a pub on the way (all this had been suggested to me by the real Nick Embiricos, whom I was trying to portray, when I visited him at his home in Sussex). Then I thought of hospitals and visiting and what I had felt when I had last visited my mother, and later my father. The bright face hiding the concern. I tried to think of this as a real hospital and imagine Nick Embiricos's attitudes to the ailing jockey on whom he relied so much.

One of the topics of earnest conversation this particular

morning had been a film shown on television the night before, called *Simon's War*, a documentary about Simon Weston of the Welsh Guards, who had been appallingly burnt and disfigured when the ship which was carrying his regiment to the Falkland Islands was hit by an Exocet missile. There were many scenes in hospital, clinical ones during examinations and operations, and emotional ones when his parents visited him. Everyone who had seen it admitted they had been moved to tears in an abundance which seldom happens. I had blubbed continuously at the misfortune and bravery of the man, at the amount of pain and suffering he had to undergo, and at the strength of his desire to get as well as he could even though he will never be able to have a proper face again.

We had also remembered, of course, that it was a film, that the lighting must have been done, and the rooms arranged and positions decided. John Irvin, who had directed documentaries in Vietnam, said that although the presence of the camera invariably affects what goes on in front of it, it does so less when events and emotions are extreme. Nevertheless, he said, it remains a great temptation for a director to ask for another take if something technical goes wrong, a temptation which Steven Rose, who had so tastefully and lovingly produced *Simon's War*, had obviously avoided.

We had noticed, too, with some despair, the immense gap that still exists between acting and real life. It is our ever present struggle to reduce that gap, by filling our minds with as much background as real-life people have, with as much imagination about the circumstances of a scene (like the shock of the parents when they first saw their broken son, but their determination to be as bright as possible and not to convey their distress to him), with a true spontaneity of speech and with a particular sort of concern with which people who love each other look at each other.

I was thinking about all this and saying to myself, "if you can be half as good as those parents were last night in their hospital ward, you'll be wonderful," when the second assistant, whose name was Peter, rushed up and said, "We're ready for you now, please," and we made our way back to the ward. The

183

noise and the banging and the talking were as insistent as ever, and it was considerably hotter. White screens had been put up against some of the windows to filter the mixture of sunlight and arclamps outside. Beds behind the camera had been taken away. There were chalk marks on the floor, one for Edward, one for me, and they were not at all where we had expected them to be. While we were waiting, Edward and I practised arriving on our marks without looking. This can take quite a little while, but it's worth persevering with because then you can forget about the mark altogether and devote yourself to the scene. It's a bit like a bowler, marking out his run up to the wicket. Then, the dialogue went something like this:

BERT: Keep the noise down. QUIET. Right, Ronnie, are you ready?

RONNIE (*after yet another look through his light-meter*): Ready. Oh, just a minute. One more minute. We need another pup. Quick, boys. Just here. That's right. Shut the left-hand side off a bit . . . er . . . OK.

BERT: All right now, Ronnie?

RONNIE (*muttering, uncertain*): Right.

BERT (*to the director*): Right, sir. (*To everyone else*) QUIET. Rehearsing. Keep them quiet in the corridor.

JOHN IRVIN: Right, let's rehearse it, please. Edward and Peter, as soon as the nurse gets to about six feet from the door you enter. Push the swing doors, let the nurse through, get to your marks and look round the room, see John, and walk towards him.

(*We go through that part of the scene.*)

JOHN IRVIN (*turning to the camera-operator, whose name is Eddie*): Any problems?

EDDIE: Er . . . Peter didn't arrive on his

184

mark so he was masked a bit by Edward . . . er . . . (*racking his brain about what he had seen through the lens only once so far: the camera-operator is the only person who actually sees what will be shown later on the screen*) and I think Peter was masked also as they came through the door; perhaps he ought to come in first . . . er . . . oh yes, and I think there's a reflection of one of the lights in the glass panel of the right-hand door as Edward opens it.

RONNIE (*abruptly*): Let's see. Yes. Damn. Damn. Er. Move that pup. It's that pup. Little more. Little more. Open the door again. That's all right.

JOHN IRVIN: So, Peter, get ahead of Edward. And you can both spend longer looking around the ward before you see John. Count of five. I'd rather have too much because then I can cut it. If there's too little I might not be able to do a cut to John when I'm editing, and I think I'd like to. One more rehearsal.

BERT: Quiet. Rehearsing.

(*We go through it again*)

JOHN IRVIN: Problems?

EDDIE: No. Much better. Er . . . I think Peter and Edward could come in a gnats earlier. It's a bit bunchy.

JOHN IRVIN: OK?

EDWARD AND ME (*together, nervous now, because we are getting so near to our first take in the film*): Yes.

JOHN IRVIN: Right, let's shoot it.

185

BERT:	Shooting next time.
	(*Ronnie walks around with his light meter, and the army of make-up and wardrobe dash up to Edward and me to dab and brush. Everybody bursts out talking. Pandemonium. The focus-puller, whose name is Cedric, comes up to us.*)
CEDRIC:	Could I see you on your marks please?
	(*Edward and I walk, still being dabbed and brushed, on to our marks. Cedric measures the distance between our faces and the lens and adjusts a knob on the side of the camera.*)
BERT:	Right, Ronnie?
RONNIE:	Right.
BERT:	Right, John?
JOHN IRVIN:	Right.
BERT:	Right. Opening positions. Thank you, gentlemen. (*Edward and I are bustled into the corridor.*) Right. Turn over.
SOUND MAN (*with earphones on, and sitting out of the way, hunched over his recording apparatus, and whose name is David*):	Just a minute, there's an aeroplane.
BERT:	Relax. Waiting for the aeroplane.
(*A great hush descends, while we all listen.*)	
BERT:	Say when, David.
DAVID:	Right.
BERT:	Here we go. Turn over.
DAVID:	Sound running.
BERT:	Mark it.
CLAPPER-LOADER (*whose name is Jason*):	143 Take 1. (*He then claps the clapper-board and scampers away and hides.*)
BERT:	Background action.

	(*The extras continue to read, or just lie there, and a nurse walks from one bed to another at the far end of the ward. Bert is responsible for all instructions to the extras.*)
JOHN IRVIN:	Action.
	(*And we do that bit of the scene.*)
JOHN IRVIN:	Cut. Good. A good one. (*He turns to Eddie, and they have a prolonged mutter, which we can't hear.*) Once more please. (*He comes up to Edward and me.*) Peter: you're just a little too ahead of Edward now. Edward, keep up with him. We lost you for a moment. I think you could be a little more ill-at-ease, Peter. Not you, Edward. Very good, both of you.
BERT:	Right, Eddie? Going again. Turn over.
DAVID:	Sound running.
JASON (*not always waiting for "Mark it"*):	143 Take 2. (*Clap. Scamper. Hide.*)
BERT:	QUIET. Background action.
JOHN IRVIN:	Action.
	(*We all do it again.*)
JOHN IRVIN:	Cut. Good. Eddie?
EDDIE:	Er . . . Peter was masked for a moment as they came through the door, and Edward stopped just a gnats too far forward. It was all right though . . . er . . .
JOHN IRVIN:	Once more.
BERT:	First positions. Thank you gentlemen. Make-up? (*Make-up dab us a bit. The heat is mounting. And the pressure.*)

187

*

And so on, through the scene, finishing with the close-ups. John's first, then Edward's, then mine. When it came to mine, John's bed had gone because the camera had to be there, and John sat next to the lens, straining his head towards it to give me the best possible eyeline. The one order which is always given to actors for close-ups is: "Watch the overlaps." This is because the microphone is adjusted only for the person who is being photographed, so nobody else's voice must coincide with his. There must be a pause before you speak and a pause after you've spoken. And problems of focus become much more acute. The director said to one of us, "Oh, yes, you can move your head about if you want to. Plenty of leeway. At least an inch."

Of course if you've done filming you will know about all this, and I rather hope you will have skipped it. I've put it in because if you *haven't* done filming it can be such a shock: the clamour, the waiting, the repetition, the exactness required, the fuss and distractions of it all. Small parts are harder to do than leading ones: if you have the lead you develop a special relationship with the director, you get to know everyone, and anyway you're always at it: there aren't those confounded and confounding days of waiting.

*

How cope with it all? First, be secure with the lines and mechanics of a scene. Then you can forget about lines and mechanics and can concentrate on the story, the situation and the people you are with. Have so much in your mind that you can, at least partially, shut out the babble and work which surround you.

"It's simply a matter of using your imagination," said John Hurt, one illuminating day. "Being real is not the aim; imagining and remembering what it's like to be ill, to be frightened of illness, to be in love, to win a race, oh, all these things with all their details, that's what to do. I don't really like using substitutions, 'as ifs', as some people call them. I like to

188

imagine what the character I'm playing wants and feels. Otherwise it's me doing the thinking, not the character. Bob Champion wanted to win the Grand National, and that's what I have to imagine if I'm going to be true to him. I'm not a method actor. I don't believe in it, really," he said. But we could see the part was taking him over and he was becoming indistinguishable from the real jockeys by whom he was surrounded. It was fascinating to watch him work. We had spent a whole day doing a scene in a crowded restaurant, and with all the people, all the lights, and the smoke-gun which was puffed for "atmosphere" before every take, there was such an oven of heat towards the end of the day that it was barely tolerable. John shut his eyes against the smoke and the heat and the deafening noise, waiting to do his close-ups. He shut out the room, and concentrated; and when the camera turned it was as though he'd never said the lines before, so fresh they were, and so immediate.

John Irvin said to me that John Hurt has a very special relationship with the camera (Alec Guinness has the same, he said), "probably because he loves it: it sees more in his face and in his eyes than I can see on the set. He often appears to be doing nothing. But he's not. The camera catches his internal life."

Years ago there was an interview with Rod Steiger in *The Times*, in which he said, "When it comes to having to do a lot of takes for a scene I try to think of them not as takes, repeating the same thing each time, but as one more opportunity to explore life in front of the camera."

Odds And Ends ∽

In a long review of *About Acting* in the *Daily Telegraph*, John Barber wrote ". . . such skills have nothing to do with great acting as I understand it." And of course he was quite right: if it were possible to give any recipes for great acting then we would all be great actors. But we're not. There are very few. It is interesting, though, that many of the Golden Rules and Helpful Hints which I included in that book came from great actors. And I've often wondered if these extraordinary people aimed to be great, or merely to be good, their greatness coming from gifts of presence, power, personality, or from beauty of face and voice. I quoted from Edith Evans more than from anybody else and I know, because she told me, that her only aim was to be a good actress: truthful, simple, but with considerable dexterity with words and moves. She didn't have a particularly beautiful face, but some inner spirit in her transformed it. She had a most idiosyncratic voice, swooping mellifluously wherever she wanted it to go, but *she* thought her speech was very real and very natural. Some are born great . . . and once they become good, God, as Prunella Scales believes, has done the rest for them.

So here, unabashed, I include some more hints and ideas, collected from various sources, and told, as before, as briefly as possible. It's a bit like playing catch: a ball is thrown in the air towards you: if you like the look of it, you can catch it, and hold it, and keep it, and make it your own; if you don't, you can let it go.

Research

Is it worth reading the novel from which the play or series is made? Is it worth reading up about a real person you're about to play? Is it worth meeting that person if you can, or watching film of them if they are famous? Is it worth finding out about the job your character has and the environment he lives in?

Of course it is. In as much detail as possible. Brian Clark, who wrote the television series *Telford's Change*, said, "I spent six months researching the whole subject of banking, both international and domestic. That six months accounted for about ten per cent of the scripts. The rest came from my head, as plays do."

But it was that ten per cent which made all the difference.

What Does Your Character Want?

What is his aim? His principle aim? His super-objective? It was Michael Denison whom I first heard use this question. He said to the author of a new play he was appearing in, "I don't know what my character wants, and until I know that he will remain a cipher to me. Can you tell me?" Unfortunately the playwright couldn't, although he was able to say quite a lot about the character's function within the play. But that's not the same thing.

What does your character want? It's a good question. You could take it further: what is your character's *obsession*?

Running Conditions

Referred to briefly earlier in this book, this phrase of Mike Leigh's is very helpful, I think. It means, of course, continuing conditions of mind or body affecting, or afflicting, the character you are playing, from, say, inordinate shyness to an itchy leg which you have to keep scratching (there was at least one in *Goose-Pimples*).

I first heard of running conditions when I was playing a character who had a particularly nasty cough. In fact the play implied he was terminally ill. During the rush of rehearsals I found what seemed to me the most convenient times for coughing, either because somebody else referred to it, or I did, or because it helped me leap more easily into sudden tempers, or because it stopped me for a moment from getting on with an urgent task. So I found the places. The only thing was, as I discovered at early previews, I was coughing far too much. The audience couldn't take it. One reviewer said that I had "a cough that even Garbo in *Camille* might have envied". It was while I was on tour with the same play (*A Coat of Varnish* by Ronald Millar) that I was told about Mike Leigh's phrase and I realised that I had not integrated the coughing into the whole performance. My running condition was an appalling chest, which hurt all the time. Not that I had to show that, I just had to know it and feel it. It made me want to control my coughing much more, because coughing was the most painful thing I could do. The upshot of all this was that I coughed much less, and in differing degrees. Much better, everybody said.

Work Till It's Easy

It was while I was on the same tour that I felt a new ease in performing, an ease I had never felt on the stage before. I think this was largely because I had rehearsed the part in March, played it for five intermittent weeks in repertory at the Haymarket Theatre, and then, after a long gap, went with it on tour in the autumn. Gaps are very helpful: the part sinks into your subconscious during the silent weeks, and when it comes to re-rehearse, emerges more freshly than you had dared to hope. I think this is because at early rehearsals you are planning what to do. You are being given a lot; you are told where to stand and sit. You spend a lot of time trying to be obedient. When you rehearse after a gap the plan is forgotten: only the story, the situations and the characters remain. If only it were possible always to throw the plan away, to forget it! I was greatly helped in this feeling of ease by being directed by Anthony Quayle and acting two of the major scenes in the play with him. We perpetually surprised each other by new readings and slightly different moves. After a performance one night I said to him, "Oh, I enjoyed it tonight. We were really acting carelessly."

And he replied, "It's a lifetime's work, learning to be careless."

Vary

People have varying views about varying their performances. But certainly the freshness and ease which I have mentioned are assisted if there is leeway, if the tracks are not too rigidly laid. It's more fun anyway, and helps prevent mechanical acting. There is nothing more boring than mechanical acting: the only thing that is interesting, for an audience, is to be in the presence of people who are thinking and feeling and not just going through the motions. Sometimes the varying can be unpremeditated. The play and the thinking about the play evolve as the performances accumulate. But sometimes, I think, it can be inspiring to carry on to the stage a new attitude, or to concentrate more than usually on some facet of the story or circumstances within the play. Do it tonight, you might say to yourself, for total personal involvement: the story *matters* to you. Do it for the job in hand (a particular favourite of mine). Do it with slightly more urgency, or slightly more awareness of the heat, or cold, or the surroundings. And most of all, do it for the other people: do it for talking and listening. Do it for speed. Do it for a little more variety. Oh, heaps of things. And when physical things change because of these changing attitudes, let them. Mustn't go too far off the rails, though, and must expect a note or two from the director when next he pays a visit.

193

Think in Pictures

Yes, in colour too. If you talk about a field, see it in your mind's eye. If you talk about an event, see it in your mind's eye.

Don't Play The Character, Play The Situation

You can't think of everything during a performance. That's what rehearsals were for, to get some of the thinking out of the way. After you've been rehearsing and playing a part for some time you can assume quite a lot. Alison Steadman knew Beverly so thoroughly towards the end of the rehearsal period that she could just switch her on. There she would be, ready, in all her outrageous detail. Then, and only then, could she concentrate on the incidents of the play. Don't play the character, play the situation.

Heels And Toes

"Have you noticed, darling," said Penelope Keith to me one evening while we were both in *Donkeys' Years*, "have you noticed how some people are heels people and other people are toes people?" I limply replied that I didn't know what she was talking about. "Well," she said, heaving herself up a little in her dressing-room chair (I had just arrived at the theatre and was paying her a visit before the show), "it's simple really, darling, but I think it's frightfully helpful when you're thinking of a character. Heels people are those who . . . you know . . ." (and she stood up to demonstrate it) ". . . sit back on their heels, go backwards like that. Shy, retiring people. Receivers, not givers. You know, backwards, not forwards. But toes people" (and she brightened her voice a little, thinking of them) "go forward and are springy and . . . giving and . . . outgoing. You know?"

"Oh yes, that is good." I said.

"M'm," she said, pleased. "I think I'm a toes person.

What do you think you are?"

"Oh . . ." I said, warily, "er . . . I'm not sure. A mixture of both, I think. I have my heels moments and my toes moments."

"Yes," she said, "perhaps you're right. But it's helpful, isn't it?"

"Very," I said.

And it is. Mind you, I think very few people are completely heels or completely toes. But a lot are mostly heels or mostly toes. It's quite nice to work out the heels moments and the toes moments of your character.

Get Rid Of Some Of It

I suppose you could say there are heels and toes playwrights too. The heels playwrights (Chekhov, for example, and in our own time Simon Gray and Alan Ayckbourn) use words which imply a large subtext: they float on top of the meaning rather than explain it, while the toes playwrights (Shakespeare and Shaw, for example, and in our own time John Osborne, Christopher Fry, David Hare and Tom Stoppard) use words to do a great deal of explaining.

It is very tempting, especially with toes playwrights, to elucidate and make the most of everything, and this can lead to an over-emphatic and therefore monotonous delivery. So: vary the emphasis. Use plus emphasis for some bits and minus emphasis for others; get rid of some of it.

For example, here's a short speech:

I had a really bad time about eleven or twelve years ago. Or thirteen, I can't remember. It was soon after I'd left school, and I could not find any purpose in my life, so I just went to pieces. I was shattered. I was tired all the time, couldn't concentrate, couldn't enjoy anything; no friends. It was awful.

Here it is again, with suggested hesitations (/) and bits to throw away (a line over the words). By no means do I think this is the only or even the best way to arrange this speech; it is just one possibility:

I had a / really / bad time about eleven or twelve
years ago. / Or thirteen, I can't remember. It was just
after I'd left school, and I could / not / find any / purpose
/in my life, so / I just went to pieces. I was shattered. I was
tired all the time, couldn't concentrate, couldn't enjoy
anything; / no friends. / It was awful.

Sometimes, if you want to go faster, you can think of the
next thing while saying the present one, and if you want to go
slower, you can become preoccupied.

These little things help.

Feelings, Not Statements

To go one stage further: you could get rid of the whole of the
following speech, feeling the heat the while, feeling listless and
tired, not making any statements.

Oh it's hot in here. Let's go out, shall we? Let's just
sit outside and get cool. Oh, the thought of being cool! The
thought of just a little air . . . There's no air in here, you
see. And perhaps we might have some tea or a drink or
something. That'll refresh us. Yes. Let's go outside.

Make Paragraphs

"Let's make some paragraphs," says the director one day.
"It's all a bit shapeless at the moment. It meanders. So let's
start here, and everybody: close the gaps between speeches, and
when we get to your line, Colin, stop. Colin's line stops you all.
He's taken you by surprise. Then, Harriet, you start the next
paragraph, and it can go pitter-patter pitter-patter for some
time . . . until . . . Colin's next line, say. Then everybody stops
again. Let's try it anyway. See if it works."

If the director has chosen well, this rehearsal can be one of
the most valuable of the lot. And then once you've got your

paragraphs with the other players firmly established, you can free them up a bit, so they don't show.

No Emotion Is Static

If you laugh, if you cry, if you are cross, if you are happy: the laughter, the crying, the rage and the joy are ever-changing. It's good to think of this, it's good to remember it: it prevents that false switch-on of artificial, because generalised, emotions. So if you laugh, you can be laughing a little more or a little less than you were a moment ago. Or a lot more (with a sudden surge) or a lot less (with a sudden collection of yourself). The worst laughter always seems to accompany the stage-direction *exeunt* at the ends of scenes in Shakespeare's comedies, usually because it has not become organic, it has not grown; it has merely been switched on because somebody said so.

Ease Into The Play

Don't tell the audience too much about your character to start with: keep some surprises in store, keep some things back. Lead the audience gently into the world of the play. Be very true to start with, then you won't put the audience off.

Edith Evans said, "When you're in a comedy, don't try for too many laughs in your first scene. The audience will tire of you, and be disappointed if you don't get funnier as the play goes on."

Hints

Nevertheless, it's nice when constructing a character to give hints, however slight, of any big changes to come. Oswald in *Ghosts* and Ophelia in *Hamlet* both go mad: the potential for madness must be there somewhere, lurking, right from the beginning; there should be a sign or two, here and there: a hint.

197

Positions And Think-Lines

Two actors are on stage, seated thus:

They sit comfortably in their chairs and talk. When they look at each other they incline their heads towards each other. When they don't look at each other, when they are thinking inside themselves, their heads return slightly towards the audience, square on their shoulders. That is their think-line. A gross simplification, this, but I've liked the idea of think-lines ever since I noticed how John Gielgud uses them a lot. Anthony Quayle does too, so I caught the habit while I was on the tour I've been talking about. He uses them off-stage as well: he looks towards you and then away, to the same place.

Recently there was a play at the National Theatre when two characters were placed sitting at a table like this:

Those two chairs gave B a most unfair advantage over A: B's natural think-line gave her plenty of command over the audience:

whereas poor A had a great deal of work to do to allow the audience sitting on the left-hand side of the auditorium to see anything of her face:

A much fairer placing would have been:

Being level with each other is not necessarily the fairest positioning: it depends where you are on the stage.

Look Around A Bit

When you have an intimate duologue, for example in a film or a television play, there is an area *around* the eyes of the other person which can attract your attention: the hair, the hairline, the brow, the mouth, the neck. Or even further away: the space *around* the other character's head. There's no need to stare each other out all the time.

From Uta Hagen

When I was in New York in the winter of 1963, I went to a class given by this remarkable actress and teacher, and three things she said that afternoon have stuck in my memory.

The first was: "When you have to be hot, or cold, or tired or whatever, don't try to be hot or cold or tired all over. Select a place, and concentrate on that. Your neck? A shoulder? The small of your back?" (Recently I saw a play called *The Dining Room* by A. R. Gurney Jr at the Greenwich Theatre. All six actors – all brilliant – had that rare opportunity of playing a lot of parts from children to very old people. When they were children they chose a few childlike – and different – things to do; when they were old, they became old because of a stiff leg, a slow walk, an aching back.)

The second was: "If you have to pull on a drawer that is supposed to be sticky, but isn't really, you can push it with your upstage hand, pull it with your downstage hand, but believe only in the downstage one."

The third was: "Try not to *tell* your acting partners what to do: *make* them. For example, if somebody has to stop you from going off the stage and they don't say the line in time, don't ask them to, just go off. They'll stop you in future."

Egg

If your speech is: "How are you today? Are you feeling

well? You look very tired," and the reply is "I'm fine," you will leave egg on your partner's face if you pause between your sentences. Yet it often seems to happen.

Actions Which Speak . . .

In the original production of *The Deep Blue Sea*, Peggy Ashcroft dropped a handkerchief. The first time I saw it I thought it was an accident. Subsequently I realised it wasn't. She stooped to pick it up, and rose wearily on I can't remember now what line, and that heavy rise was an encapsulation of the weariness inside her.

Additional Words

I am often tempted – and fall to the temptation – to add "Well," or "Oh," or "And," or something to the beginning of an author's line. Sometimes the author has asked me not to, but I think a little licence is legitimate. However, sometimes (notably on television) the additions become incredibly complex, time-wasting and very boring to listen to. They can grow like this:

"Look . . ."
"Look, Nigel . . ."
"Yes, well . . ."
"Well, yes, but I mean . . ."
"Yes, well, but Nigel, look . . ."
"Oh, well, no, but Nigel, look . . ."
"Oh, well, yes, I mean, but Nigel, look . . ."
"Well yes, but you know, Nigel, I mean to say, look . . ."

Off-Form

You can be off-form for a performance, for a string of

performances, for a whole play, or, indeed, for a whole period. Everybody has their off-form times . . . you've only got to look at the very famous sports people.

I remember watching, on Italian television, a men's singles tennis championship. Although I couldn't understand a word of the commentary, it was easy to tell which player was winning and which was losing. The winning player, quietly confident, showed little emotion, and between rallies he stared at his opponent, or at his racket, which he twirled gently around. The losing player, who couldn't concentrate any more, gasped with indignation at his every mistake, and between shots looked around at the crowd and the cameras, and then tried to pull himself together.

One was relaxed, the other was tense. Oh, we've all seen it; and we've all felt it too.

Take The Hurdles As They Come

Yes, a loser anticipates disaster, working himself into a lather of uncertainty before each shot, and sure as eggs, disaster occurs. He who hesitates . . .

I was beginning to froth a bit before the transmission of a "live" television play, going over bits and pieces which had always worried me. It was a two-hander, and my partner was Charles Gray, who said to me, very quietly, a few minutes before we went on the air, "Don't worry it . . . don't fuss it . . . take the hurdles as they come." I felt immensely calmed by that, and often think of it now.

Maxims ~

As you get older you remain exactly the same, only more so.

The good things get better, the bad things get worse.

There is no substitute for repetition.

Don't expect praise.

Don't ask for opinions.

You can't make anybody love you.

It's easier to act with people you like.

Confidence and concentration go hand in hand.

Every part is a character part, but should look a straight one.

A good performance is one in which the actor seems to be conceiving the words and not merely remembering them.

Put a bit of mess in.

Everything is habit-forming.

Do remember to forget
Anger, worry and regret.

Play your character from the character's point of view.

It isn't the time spent learning that matters, it's the time spent having learnt.

Say yes only if you want to.

Say no only when you have to.

You employ your agent.

Try to bring to every part something you've never thought of before.

Never stop looking – at people and things.

203

How you start in a play is more important than how you finish, because it is then that an audience makes up its mind about you.

Don't use more energy for an action than the action requires.

In every company find a chum.

If two people are whispering and looking at you, don't assume they are talking about you; and, if they are, don't assume that what they are saying is bad.

Don't try to impress people.

Don't plunge in at the deep end if you don't know the pool.

Hard work never killed anybody.

Be absurdly generous.

You can't please everyone.

You can't worry and think.

The first duty of an actor is to be heard.

Vowels travel easily, consonants don't.

Acting is giving; reticence has no part in it.

Mechanical acting just won't do.

(and, from a letter written by Edward Fitzgerald):

At all cost, a thing must live: better a live sparrow than a stuffed eagle.

Index

Entries in *Italic* refer to an interview by the author.

208